THE WI   F
PASTRY

JANET WIER

EBURY
PRESS

ACKNOWLEDGEMENTS

Illustrated by Cooper-West Graphic Design
Edited by Sue Jacquemier and Rosemary Wadey
Designed by Clare Clements
Cover photography by John Lee

ISBN 0 85223 322 1

Published by Ebury Press
National Magazine House
72 Broadwick Street
London W1V 2BP

First impression 1984

Filmset by
D. P. Media Limited, Hitchin, Hertfordshire

Reproduced, printed and bound in Great Britain by
Hazell Watson & Viney Limited,
Member of the BPCC Group,
Aylesbury, Bucks

CONTENTS

INTRODUCTION

There is a real art to making good pastry, but it is one that can easily be mastered if a few simple rules are followed. Patience is essential; so too is the all-important 'light touch' necessary when making pastry. The 'feel' of the pastry is governed mainly by the amount of liquid added, but the lightness is achieved by incorporating air – either by rubbing the fat into the flour, or by folding and rolling to catch air between the layers of dough or by beating it in as in the case of choux pastry.

Treat pastry gently and lightly; do not pull or stretch it or throw it around, and above all use the fingertips. Keep everything cool, both the ingredients and the implements, and do allow the pastry time to relax before rolling out.

It is often better to dust the pastry board with cornflour rather than flour; it is very light and silky and does not unbalance the recipe by adding more flour to it than is necessary.

Most pastries call for plain flour, the exception being suet crust. However, some people have their own versions of the basic pastries which may contain a proportion of self-raising flour and they will swear their pastry is the best around – it may be good, but it will not beat a well-made true basic pastry.

Many recipes in this book call for the pastry to be cooked on baking sheets lined with baking paper. This will prevent sticking and ensure ease of movement but is not strictly necessary. A damp or lightly greased baking sheet may also be used.

Pastry trimmings can be utilized by cutting them into pastry leaves, circles, diamonds etc., glazing them with beaten egg or milk and cooking them on a shelf under the main dish. They can then be frozen and used for garnishes to soups and stews and as party nibbles.

How to use this book

This book is organised into seven chapters; at the beginning of each one is an introduction giving hints and tips related to the subject of the chapter. Inexperienced cooks are advised to read the introduction before beginning a recipe in that chapter.

The basic recipes at the start of each chapter are referred to later in the chapter and elsewhere in the book. Techniques are sometimes referred to in recipes and are fully explained elsewhere in the book, normally in the introduction. Usually they are cross-referenced, but if you find an unfamiliar term with no cross-reference, look it up in the index to find the page with the explanation.

In each chapter, there are sweet and savoury dishes; the savoury recipes are grouped near the beginning of each chapter, and the sweet ones towards the end. Use the index to find recipes for specific ingredients, such as chicken or chocolate.

Measurements

All the spoon measures in this book are level unless stated otherwise.

3 tsp = 1 tbsp
8 tbsp = 5 fl oz = 150 ml = ¼ pint

Eggs are taken to be size 2 unless stated otherwise.

When following these recipes please use either the metric measurements or the imperial; do not mix them and then all will be well.

When a recipe states '175 g (6 oz) pastry' it means pastry made using 175 g (6 oz) flour. It does not mean 175 g (6 oz) prepared pastry.

Measurements for can sizes are approximate.

American equivalents

	Metric	Imperial	American
Butter, margarine	225 g	8 oz	1 cup
Shredded suet	100 g	4 oz	1 cup
Flour	100 g	4 oz	1 cup
Currants	150 g	5 oz	1 cup
Sugar	200 g	7 oz	1 cup
Syrup	335 g	11½ oz	1 cup

An American pint is 16 fl oz compared with the imperial pint of 20 fl oz. A standard American cup measure is considered to hold 8 fl oz.

To line a flan ring

Put the flan ring on baking paper on an oven tray.

Roll the pastry out on a cornfloured board to a thickness of 5 mm (¼ inch) and 5 cm (2 inches) larger than the ring.

Lift it on the rolling pin. Slip it off over the ring and push into place, without stretching it, using a little ball of pastry. Roll across the top of the ring with the rolling pin to cut off overhanging pastry.

To bake blind

Preheat the oven to 200°C (400°F) mark 6 for short crust and most flan pastries, and 220°C (425°F) mark 7 for flaky pastry. Line the flan ring or oven-proof dish with pastry rolled out to a thickness of about 5 mm (¼ inch). Poke down into the dish using a little ball of the pastry as a pusher.

Line with greaseproof paper and fill with baking beans or any other beans. Bake for 15 minutes, remove the beans and paper. Bake for a further 10 minutes to dry out (less for tartlets).

Baking a flan case 'blind' makes it easy to turn out of the case or ring.

To cover a pie

Roll out the pastry 5 cm (2 inches) larger than the dish. Cut off a strip all around, 2.5 cm (1 inch) wide. Brush the rim of the pie dish with water. Fit on the pastry strip. Brush with water. (One wet and one dry surface of pastry stick together better than two wet surfaces.) Lift the remaining piece of pastry on the rolling pin and transfer to the filled dish. Press the edges firmly together and trim. Knock up the edges and flute (see below).

Knocking up and fluting

'Knocking up' is making horizontal cuts with the back of a knife along the edge of the pastry. These cuts release it so it can rise. 'Fluting' is decorating the edge of pastry by pinching or by using a fork for savoury dishes (the tip of the spoon for sweet dishes).

Fluted edge

Edge decorated with a fork

Knocked up edge

Freezing

Pastry cases freeze very well but are fragile when frozen so need careful handling. Thaw before filling and cooking. If the filling is to be cold or uncooked, crisp the flan case in the oven before using it.

SHORT CRUST PASTRY

Short crust pastry is very versatile, as the recipes in this chapter show. It can be used for meat and fruit pies and tarts, but also for things like sausage rolls and apricot turnovers.

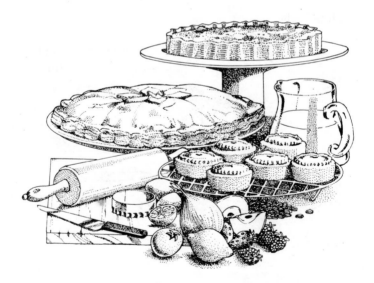

The most popular and useful of all pastries. It gets its name from the short fibres developed during the light, cool 'rubbing in'.

Handle the pastry as little as possible and roll it with short light strokes. A dusting of cornflour on the pin and the board is better than flour (never dust the pastry). Half lard and half margarine with plain flour makes the crispest pastry.

Pastry made with wholemeal flour, or a proportion of wholemeal flour, can be used for all the short crust recipes in this chapter. Follow the basic recipe, though do not make the startling mistake of sieving wholemeal flour before using it. This is a real 'country' pastry. There is also now on the market some excellent brown self-raising flour which makes delicious scones, dumplings and suet puddings. Pastas can be made with brown flour too.

A basic, very simple, recipe for cheese pastry is also included in this chapter.

SHORT CRUST PASTRY

225 g (8 oz) plain flour
¼ tsp salt
50 g (2 oz) margarine
50 g (2 oz) lard
about 3 tbsp cold water

Sieve the flour and salt into a bowl. Add the fats and rub in gently and lightly. Mix to a stiff dough with the water (if the dough is too wet the pastry will be tough). Knead very lightly and handle as little as possible. Roll out evenly and lightly.

WHOLEMEAL SHORT CRUST PASTRY

225 g (8 oz) wholemeal flour
50 g (2 oz) lard
50 g (2 oz) margarine
½ tsp salt
about 4 tbsp water

Mix the salt into the flour with your fingertips. Rub in the fats until the mixture resembles breadcrumbs. This takes longer but try to do it lightly. Add the water, cut and stir with a knife until the mixture starts to bind. Gather into a ball with the fingertips and roll out on a board lightly dredged with cornflour.

This is naturally a rather crumbly pastry because of the large particles in the flour. You might prefer to make a start with 85% extraction flour, and see how it goes. Alternatively use half wholemeal flour and half plain white flour.

HOMEMADE MAYONNAISE

2 egg yolks
½ tsp made mustard
275 ml (½ pint) oil
1 tbsp lemon juice
2–3 tbsp vinegar (wine, cider or
    white)
1 tsp caster sugar
salt and pepper

Put the egg yolks and mustard into a warmed bowl and mix thoroughly. Whisk in half the oil, drop by drop, using a hand or electric whisk, until thick. Add the lemon juice and then continue with the remainder of the oil. Add vinegar, sugar and seasonings to taste and store in a screw-topped jar or airtight container in the refrigerator.

Homemade mayonnaise will keep well for at least two weeks in the refrigerator.

Always use eggs at room temperature; if taken straight out of the refrigerator, the mayonnaise may well curdle.

SIMPLE CHEESE PASTRY

175 g (6 oz) plain flour
salt and cayenne pepper
½ tsp mustard powder
75 g (3 oz) butter
100 g (4 oz) grated cheese
1 egg yolk
a little water

Mix the flour, mustard, and seasonings well together with the fingertips. Rub in the butter, then mix in the cheese. Add the egg yolk and a little water if necessary to mix to a firm but pliable dough. Cover and leave to relax. Use as required.

Cook at 200°C (400°F) mark 6.

This is a cheese straw mixture and is also used for Garlic Salé (see page 14).

SIMPLE BÉCHAMEL SAUCE

Makes approx. 275 ml (½ pint)

1 blade mace
1 bay leaf
6 peppercorns
2 slices onion
275 ml (½ pint) milk
25 g (1 oz) butter
25 g (1 oz) plain flour
salt and pepper

Infuse the mace, bay leaf, peppercorns and onion in the milk over a low heat with the lid on, for 10 minutes. Melt the butter in a pan. Add the flour and stir well over a low heat for a minute or so. Strain the milk and add slowly to the flour and butter mixture, beating all the time until boiling.

Simmer slowly for 20 minutes, stirring now and then, to ensure a velvety, well-flavoured sauce. Season to taste.

LAMB AND KIDNEY PASTIES

Makes 6

350 g (12 oz) short crust pastry (see page 9)
175 g (6 oz) lean boneless lamb
3 lamb's kidneys
75 g (3 oz) mushrooms
2 tbsp water
salt and pepper
the smallest pinch of powdered rosemary
1 egg to glaze

Heat the oven to 200°C (400°F) mark 6. Roll out the pastry and, using a large plain cutter or saucer, cut out six circles. Release from the board and leave to relax.

Cut the meat into small dice. Skin, split and core the kidneys and cut into quarters. Wipe and slice the mushrooms. Put all these ingredients into a bowl with the water, salt and pepper to taste and the rosemary, and mix well.

Divide the filling between the pastry rounds. Brush one half of the circle with beaten egg and bring up the edges to meet each other at the top. Press well together and flute (see page 7). Brush the pasties with beaten egg, place on a baking sheet and cook for 30 minutes. Reduce the temperature to 180°C (350°F) mark 4 and continue for 20–25 minutes. Serve hot or cold.

RABBIT IN A BLANKET

Serves 8 hungry people

1 kg (2½ lb) young rabbit
225 g (8 oz) streaky bacon
1 tsp mixed dried herbs
salt and ground black pepper
675 g (1½ lb) short crust pastry (see page 9)
350 g (12 oz) pork sausagemeat
2 hard-boiled eggs
1 egg to glaze

Heat the oven to 200°C (400°F) mark 6. Joint and bone the rabbit (very easy). Rind the bacon, cut out any white bone and cut into strips. Mix with the rabbit meat and sprinkle with the herbs, salt and pepper.

Roll out the pastry to a circle approximately 44 cm (16 inches) across and put it carefully on to a baking sheet. Cut the pastry into the form of a broad cross. Mark a 25-cm (10-inch) square in the middle and extend the sides to the edge of the pastry. Cut away the 'triangles'. Spread half the sausagemeat on to the square piece in the middle. Arrange the rabbit mixture on top of it. Slice the hard-boiled eggs on top of that, and finish with the other half of the sausagemeat; spread flat.

Brush alternate edges of the pastry with beaten egg, and draw the square flaps up to meet over the rabbit. Pinch edges firmly together and flute with finger and thumb (see page 7). Make a little hole in the top to let the steam out. Brush the 'blanket' all over with beaten egg. Make some pastry leaves from the pastry trimmings and place around the hole; glaze with egg. Bake for 40 minutes then reduce the temperature to 180°C (350°F) mark 4 and continue for another hour. Cover with greaseproof paper when the pastry is sufficiently browned.

Do put the pastry on the baking sheet before you start rolling. This is a very easy dish to make. Take your time and enjoy it. Rabbit in a Blanket is good cold if a jelly filling is put in when the pie has cooled; allow to set overnight. Bought aspic jelly is delicious for this. It 'matches' well, and is a great time-saver.

CUCUMBER AND CHICKEN CUPS

Makes 14

175 g (6 oz) short crust pastry (see page 9)
about 350 g (12 oz) cooked white chicken meat
¼ cucumber
tbsp homemade mayonnaise (see page 10)
salt and pepper
watercress to garnish

Heat the oven to 200°C (400°F) mark 6. Roll out the pastry to a thickness of 5 mm (¼ inch). Cut out 14 rounds using a fluted cutter to suit the deepest patty pans you have. Line the tins and bake blind (see page 6). Cool on a wire rack.

Cut the chicken meat into 1-cm (½-inch) cubes. Dice the cucumber (do not peel it). Fold both into the mayonnaise. Season, and use to fill the tartlets.

Serve very cold, topped with a small sprig of watercress.

CHEESE AND APPLE PIE

Serves 4–6

175 g (6 oz) short crust pastry (see
  page 9)
100 g (4 oz) cheese
100 g (4 oz) sugar
¼ tsp salt
25 g (1 oz) flour
¼ tsp nutmeg
grated rind of 1 lemon
450 g (1 lb) cooking apples
milk to glaze
caster sugar

Heat the oven to 200°C (400°F) mark 6.
Dice the cheese into a basin, add the sugar,
salt, flour, grated nutmeg and lemon rind.
Mix them all well.

Roll out the pastry to a thickness of 5 mm
(¼ inch). Line a 500-ml (1-pint) pie dish
and trim the edge. Peel, core and slice the
apples and use some to cover the bottom of
the lined pie dish. Add half the cheese
mixture and then another layer of apples
and the remaining cheese. Finish with a
layer of apples. Turn in the pastry edge to
just overlap the fruit. Brush with milk. Roll
out the pastry trimmings, cut into thin
strips and use to lattice the top of the pie.
Brush the pastry with milk and dust with
caster sugar. Wipe the pie dish edge clean.

Stand on a baking sheet and cook for
25 minutes. Cover with greaseproof paper
and cook for a further 15 minutes.

Lancashire cheese is *the* cheese for melting.
It has a wonderfully subtle taste and melts
into a thick cream. It is renowned for its
splended toasting qualities, and is perfect
for this North Country tart.

GARLIC SALÉ

Serves 4

175 g (6 oz) cheese pastry (see page
  11)
275 ml (½ pint) béchamel sauce (see
  page 11), cooled
3 eggs
150 g (5 oz) grated garlic cheese
a grate or two of nutmeg

Heat the oven to 200°C (400°F) mark 6. Roll
out the pastry and use to line an 18-cm
(7-inch) ovenproof flan dish. Bake blind
(see page 6).

Beat the eggs into the cool sauce followed
by the cheese. Pour into the pastry case,
grate a little nutmeg over it and cook for
about 30 minutes until well browned.

HARVEST SAUSAGE ROLLS

Makes 10–14, depending on size

225 g (8 oz) wholemeal short crust
    pastry (see page 10)
1 egg (size 5 or 6)
½ tsp dried sage
225 g (8 oz) pork sausagemeat
25 g (1 oz) bran

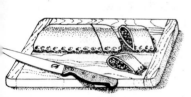

Heat the oven to 200°C (400°F) mark 6. Roll out half the pastry in a strip about 20 x 10 cm (11 x 4 inches). Do the same with the other half. Leave the strips to relax.

Beat the egg and mix half of it into the sausagemeat with the sage. Wash and dry your hands and dust in wholemeal flour. Mould the sausagemeat into two rolls. Put one on each of the strips of pastry. Brush beaten egg along one edge of each and fold over. Press the edges firmly together. Brush each roll with beaten egg and sprinkle with bran. Cut diagonally to make individual sausage rolls. Put on a baking sheet and bake for 20–30 minutes. Cool on a wire rack.

Eat hot or cold. Homemade mustard (see page 74) makes these special sausage rolls even more delicious.

SAVOURY FLAN

Serves 4–5

175 g (6 oz) short crust pastry (see
    page 9)
25 g (1 oz) butter
25 g (1 oz) plain flour
275 ml (½ pint) milk
1 tsp chopped parsley
100 g (4 oz) grated cheese
3 hard-boiled eggs, sliced
50 g (2 oz) shelled prawns
salt and pepper
parsley to garnish

Heat the oven to 200°C (400°F) mark 6. Roll out the pastry to a thickness of 5 mm (¼ inch) and use to line a 20 or 23-cm (8 or 9-inch) fireproof dish or flan ring. Bake blind (see page 6).

Make the parsley sauce: melt the butter in a pan, add the flour and heat well over a low heat. Remove from the heat. Add the milk little by little, beating all the time. Return to the heat and bring slowly to the boil, stirring continuously. Cook for a minute or two. Add the cheese, eggs, prawns and 1 teaspoon parsley. Bring back to nearly boiling point and season to taste. Pour into the hot pastry case and serve at once, garnished with a small sprig of parsley.

CURD CHEESE CAKE

Serves 6

175 g (6 oz) short crust pastry (see page 9)
25 g (1 oz) currants
1 egg, beaten
25 g (1 oz) butter
225 g (8 oz) curd cheese
50 g (2 oz) soft brown sugar
grated rind of 1 lemon

Heat the oven to 190°C (375°F) mark 5 with a baking sheet in it. Roll out the pastry to a thickness of 5 mm (¼ inch). Leave to relax while you wash the currants. Melt the butter in a saucepan, add the currants, beaten egg, cheese, sugar and grated lemon rind. Stir well and set aside.

Line a 15 or 18-cm (6 or 7-inch) fluted porcelain ovenproof dish with the pastry and trim off with the rolling pin. Pour the cheese mixture into the pastry case. Cook on the hot baking sheet for 40 minutes.

The inexperienced cook will realize the enormous advantage of not having to turn out this cheese cake. These beautiful white dishes have saved many a kitchen panic.

APRICOT TURNOVERS

Makes 10

225 g (8 oz) dried apricots
50 g (2 oz) apricot jam
1 tbsp ground almonds
grated rind and juice of 1 lemon
225 g (8 oz) short crust pastry (see page 9)
milk to glaze
a few flaked almonds
caster sugar

Soak the apricots overnight. Heat the oven to 200°C (400°F) mark 6. Strain the apricots, discarding the water. Cut them up and mix with the jam, ground almonds, lemon rind and juice.

Roll out the pastry to a rectangle approximately 50 x 20 cm (20 x 8 inches) and trim the edges. Cut in half lengthwise and again into pieces about 10 cm (4 inches) square. Turn the squares over and brush two edges with water or milk. Put 2 teaspoons of the apricot mixture on each and fold the pastry over corner to corner. Press edges together, brush with milk, sprinkle a few flaked almonds on each and lightly dredge with caster sugar. Cook for 30 minutes. Cover with greaseproof paper if the almonds brown too quickly.

STRAWBERRY TARTLETS

Makes 16–20

225 g (8 oz) short crust pastry (see
  page 9)
450 g (1 lb) strawberries
225 g (8 oz) strawberry jam
1 tbsp water

Heat the oven to 200°C (400°F) mark 6. Roll out the pastry to a thickness of 5 mm (¼ inch). Release from the board with a palette knife and leave to relax for 10 minutes. Lightly grease the tartlet tins. Cut out 16–20 rounds of pastry with a fluted cutter a little larger than the tins. Flip over and line the tins with the pastry. Bake blind (see page 6). Cool before taking out of tins.

Arrange the fruit in the tartlets, points uppermost. Put the jam and water into a pan and simmer, stirring gently. Rub through a sieve or whizz up in a blender. Spoon carefully over the fruit in the tartlets and leave to set.

End-of-season jam strawberries are ideal.

PLATE APPLE PIE

Serves 4

225 g (8 oz) short crust pastry (see
  page 9)
450 g (1 lb) cooking apples
50 g (2 oz) brown sugar
2 tbsp apricot jam
25 g (1 oz) butter
1 egg white
caster sugar

Heat the oven to 200°C (400°F) mark 6. Peel, core and slice the apples. Mix in a bowl with the sugar, apricot jam and butter.

Cut the pastry in half. Roll out one half and use to line the base of an 18 or 20-cm (7 or 8-inch) enamel plate. Put the prepared fruit on the lined plate. Brush the edge of the pastry with lightly beaten egg white. Roll out the other half of the pastry and use to cover the pie. Press the edges firmly together, knock-up and flute (see page 7). Make three slashes across the top (to let the steam out). Brush with the rest of the beaten egg white and sprinkle lightly with caster sugar. Bake for 40 minutes.

Apples shrink in cooking, so crowd them in. Apricot jam is a perfect match for apples.

TREACLE TART

Serves 4

*175 g (6 oz) short crust pastry (see
    page 9)
175 g (6 oz) golden syrup
75 g (3 oz) fresh brown
    breadcrumbs
grated rind and juice of 1 lemon*

Heat the oven to 200°C (400°F) mark 6. Roll
out the pastry and use to line an 18-cm
(7-inch) fluted ovenproof china dish. Warm
the syrup and add the breadcrumbs. Add
the rind and juice from the lemon to the
syrup. Spoon the mixture into the pastry
case.

Roll out the pastry left-overs. Cut into
strips, twist, and use to make a lattice over
the tart. Cook for 30 minutes. Best served
cold with cream.

This tart, as all open tarts, can be made and
cooked on a plate. An old enamel one from
your mother's kitchen will cook a much
better tart than a smart new ovenproof glass
one. The metal is a sharp conductor of heat
so the bottom is always cooked.

GRAPE AND LIME TART

Serves 4

*225 g (8 oz) short crust pastry (see
    page 9)
1 packet lime jelly
450 g (1 lb) green grapes
1 lime*

Heat the oven to 200°C (400°F) mark 6.
Make the jelly using 50 ml (2 fl oz) water
less than the directions suggest. Peel and
de-pip the grapes (a hair-pin makes a super
gadget for this).

Roll the pastry out to a thickness of 5 mm
(¼ inch) and use to line a 20 or 23-cm (8 or
9-inch) fluted ovenproof dish. Bake blind
(see page 6). Put the grapes, when cool, in
circles on the pastry. Grate the zest from the
lime, squeeze the juice and add both to the
jelly. Stir, and spoon the jelly carefully over
the grapes. Allow to set and serve with
cream.

A Swiss roll tin could be used for this. The
tart should then be turned out – tricky.

MINCE PIES

Makes 12

225 g (8 oz) short crust pastry (see
  page 9)
350 g (12 oz) mincemeat
milk to glaze
caster sugar

Heat the oven to 200°C (400°F) mark 6. Roll out the pastry and cut out rounds with a fluted cutter to fit the patty pans. Roll out the remaining pastry and trimmings, and with a plain cutter, cut 12 rounds a little larger than the patty tins (pastry shrinks as it is cooked). Flip them over and use to line the tins. Spoon mincemeat into each. Brush the plain edges with milk and cover with the fluted tops. Make a little hole in the top of each pie, brush with milk and dust with sugar. Cook on a baking sheet for 20–25 minutes.

Fluted tops at least one size smaller than the little pans can be used. They sit on top of the mincemeat, look very attractive and do away with a mouthful or two of pastry for those to whom such things are of concern.

RAISIN AND CIDER TART

Serves 6

175 g (6 oz) short crust pastry (see
  page 9)
350 g (12 oz) stoned raisins, washed
  and drained
1 tbsp cornflour
275 ml (½ pint) cider
25 g (1 oz) brown sugar
milk to glaze
demerara sugar

Heat the oven to 200°C (400°F) mark 6. Blend the cornflour with a little cider. Put it with the remaining cider, raisins and brown sugar into a saucepan. Bring slowly to the boil, stirring all the time. Cook for 1 minute, then cool.

Cut the pastry in half. Roll out one piece and use to line a 23-cm (9-inch) ovenproof plate. Turn the mixture onto the pastry. Brush the edge of the pastry with milk.

Roll out the second piece and use to cover the tart. Press the edges firmly together, knock-up and flute (see page 7). Make two slanting cuts in the top, brush with milk and sprinkle lightly with demerara sugar. Bake for 30 minutes.

FLAN PASTRIES

This chapter includes five different basic flan pastries, and recipes using fish, meat, vegetables and fruit, as well as some special party dishes.

Flan pastries are richer than short crust pastry, having a higher proportion of fat and often beaten egg, egg yolks and milk as the binding agents. They are quite fragile to handle and benefit from chilling before rolling out to help ease the process. When cooked, the pastry should be thin and crisp.

All the basic recipes in this chapter (apart from the lemon pastry) are made in the French way. This involves sieving the flour and salt together and then making a well in the centre. The fat, eggs and sugar (for sweet pastry) are put into the well and after mixing together the flour is gradually drawn in with the fingertips. As with all pastry, success is gained by a light, gentle touch, use of fingertips only and keeping everything cool. Do not be tempted to over-knead, as this only makes tough pastry.

PÂTE BRISÉE

225 g (8 oz) plain flour
good pinch of salt
75 g (3 oz) butter
1 egg (size 3 or 4)
125 ml (scant ¼ pint) water

Sieve the flour and salt together and make a well in the centre. Put the butter, egg and water into the well. Mix well together with the tips of the fingers, then gradually draw the flour down into the mixture, mixing as lightly as possible until all is incorporated.

Knead the dough for a minute, then roll the pastry into a ball, cover and leave to cool and relax for 1–2 hours.

Cook at 200°C (400°F) mark 6.

RICH SHORT CRUST PASTRY (ENGLISH FLAN)

225 g (8 oz) plain flour
pinch of salt
150 g (5 oz) butter
2 egg yolks
a little cold water if needed

Sieve the flour and salt into a bowl and rub in the butter. Beat the egg yolks. Make a well in the flour, add the egg yolks and mix well. Gradually draw down the flour from the sides and work it all in with the tips of the fingers. It should be a firm yet soft dough, so add a teaspoon or two of cold water if necessary. Cover and leave to cool and relax.
Cook at 200°C (400°F) mark 6.

PÂTE SUCRÉE (SWEET FLAN PASTRY)

Add 25 g (1 oz) sieved icing sugar or caster sugar to the dry ingredients in either of the basic recipes already mentioned (pâte brisée or rich short crust pastry).

PÂTE FROLLE (ALMOND PASTRY)

225 g (8 oz) plain flour
75 g (3 oz) ground almonds
1 egg
75 g (3 oz) caster sugar
100 g (4 oz) butter
1 drop almond essence

Sieve the flour into a bowl. Sprinkle the ground almonds over the flour. Make a well in the centre and break the egg into the well. Add the sugar, butter and essence. Mix with the fingertips, then start drawing the flour down gradually until all is incorporated and the pastry made. Roll into a ball, cover and leave to cool and relax in the refrigerator for an hour or two.
Cook at 190°C (375°F) mark 5.

This is baked at a slightly cooler temperature because any nut pastry 'catches' easily because of the extra oil in the nuts.

LEMON PASTRY

100 g (4 oz) butter
50 g (2 oz) caster sugar
1 egg yolk
grated rind and juice of 1 lemon
175 g (6 oz) plain flour

Cream the butter and sugar until light and white. Break in the egg yolk. Add the lemon rind and juice to the mixture and beat well.

Sieve the flour and fold lightly into the mixture. Form into a ball with the fingertips. Cover and put into the refrigerator for an hour or two before using. Cook at 200°C (400°F) mark 6.

APRICOT GLAZE

100 g (4 oz) apricot jam
100 g (4 oz) sugar
150 ml (¼ pint) water

Put the jam, sugar and water in a pan. Gently dissolve the sugar. Bring to the boil, and boil to reduce to almost half the quantity. Sieve. Reheat. Always use a glaze boiling hot for glazing fruit.

This glaze will keep for some weeks in a screw-top jar.

SMOKED COD'S ROE TARTLETS

Makes about 12

175 g (6 oz) pâte brisée or rich short crust pastry (see pages 21–2)
100 g (4 oz) smoked cod's roe
1 hard-boiled egg
a few stuffed olives

Heat the oven to 200°C (400°F) mark 6. Roll out the pastry very lightly and cut into rounds about 9 cm (3½ inches) across with a fluted cutter. Line patty tines with the pastry. Cut out rounds of greaseproof paper and line the tarts. Bake blind (see page 6) for 15 minutes. Remove the paper and beans and bake for another 5 minutes or so. Cool on a wire rack.

Skin the roe and mash with a fork. Chop the hard-boiled egg as finely as possible and fold into the roe. Fill the pastry cases very neatly with the mixture, and top with a slice of stuffed olive.

These tartlets are useful either as a 'starter' or as a savoury at the end of a meal.

SMOKED HADDOCK FLAN

Serves 4–6

225 g (8 oz) pâte brisée or rich short crust pastry (see pages 21–2)
450 g (1 lb) smoked haddock
275 ml (½ pint) milk
2 hard-boiled eggs
25 g (1 oz) butter
25 g (1 oz) plain flour
2 tbsp chopped parsley

Heat the oven to 200°C (400°F) mark 6. Roll out the pastry and use to line a 20-cm (8-inch) fluted ovenproof china flan dish. Bake blind (see page 6). Increase oven temperature to 220°C (425°F) mark 7.

Simmer the haddock in the milk until tender. Remove the fish and keep the milk. Carefully flake the fish, discarding every scrap of bone and skin. Chop the eggs and add to the fish.

Make a parsley sauce: melt the butter in a pan, add the flour and cook for 1 minute. Gradually add the reserved milk and bring up to the boil, beating all the time. Stir in the parsley and then fold in the fish and egg mixture. Fill the flan case with the mixture. Stand the dish on a baking sheet and cook for 20 minutes or until browned.

PORK ENVELOPES

Makes 4–5

225 g (8 oz) pâte brisée or rich short
  crust pastry (see pages 21–2)
100 g (4 oz) pork fillet
25 g (1 oz) dried apricots
50 g (2 oz) mushrooms
50 g (2 oz) dripping
½ tsp dried sage
salt and pepper
150 ml (¼ pint) béchamel sauce (see
  page 11)
milk to glaze

Heat the oven to 200°C (400°F) mark 6. Roll out the pastry and cut into four 12.5-cm (5-inch) squares. Leave to relax.

Dice the pork fillet. Wash the apricots and snip them into small pieces. Wipe and dice the mushrooms. Sauté the pork in the dripping until tender. Add the apricots and mushrooms and cook for a further 1–2 minutes. Stir in the sage, season well and remove from the heat. Bind together with the béchamel sauce. Spoon on to the middle of the squares.

Brush two sides of each square with water. Bring the corners up to meet in the middle. Press together firmly and flute. Make a leaf or two from the pastry trimmings. Brush with milk and cook until well browned for about 20–30 minutes.

DEVILLED KIDNEY PASTIES

Makes 4–5

225 g (8 oz) pâte brisée or rich short
  crust pastry (see pages 21–2)
4 lamb's kidneys
2 shallots
1 carrot
approx 150 ml (¼ pint) brown stock
1 bay leaf
pepper and salt
½ tsp homemade mustard (see
  page 74)
25 g (1 oz) fresh brown
  breadcrumbs
1 tsp tomato purée
milk to glaze

Heat the oven to 200°C (400°F) mark 6. Roll out the pastry and cut four circles using a saucer about 15 cm (6 inches) in diameter as a guide. Leave to relax.

Skin, core and quarter the kidneys. Peel and dice the shallots and carrot. Put in a pan with the brown stock and the bay leaf. Season well. Simmer until the kidneys are tender. Stir in the mustard, breadcrumbs and purée. Simmer until thick, then cool.

Spoon the mixture into the middle of each pastry circle. Brush half the edges with water. Bring the sides up to the top and press firmly together. Flute with finger and thumb (see page 7). Brush with milk to glaze. Stand on a baking sheet and cook for about 20 minutes until golden brown.

SWEETBREAD FLAN

Serves 4

225 g (8 oz) pâte brisée or rich short
    crust pastry (see pages 21–2)
450 g (1 lb) lamb's sweetbreads
4 tbsp mixed diced vegetables
sprig of thyme
15 g (½ oz) butter
15 g (½ oz) plain flour
salt and black pepper
4 medium mushrooms to garnish
parsley sprigs to garnish ·

Heat the oven to 200°C (400°F) mark 6.
Line an 18-cm (7-inch) flan case with the
pastry and bake blind (see page 6).

Wash the sweetbreads. Put into boiling
water for a minute or two. Drain. Trim and
cut off the gristly bits. Put the sweetbreads
into a pan with the mixed diced vegetables
and thyme. Barely cover with water and
simmer for 40 minutes. Drain the
sweetbreads and vegetables and discard the
thyme, reserving the liquor.

Make a sauce: heat the butter in a pan.
Add the flour and stir well for a minute or
so. Gradually add 150 ml (¼ pint) cooking
liquor, beating all the time; bring to the
boil. Taste and season.

Add the sweetbreads and vegetables to
the sauce. Reheat and fill the warm flan case
with the mixture. Garnish with very finely
sliced raw mushrooms (use a mandolin) and
a small sprig or two of parsley. Serve hot.

COURGETTE QUICHE

Serves 4

225 g (8 oz) pâte brisée or rich short
    crust pastry (see pages 21–2)
oil
1 onion, finely chopped
450 g (1 lb) courgettes, thinly sliced
salt and pepper
3 eggs
150 ml (¼ pint) milk
100 g (4 oz) finely grated cheese

Heat the oven to 200°C (400°F) mark 6.
Line a 20-cm (8-inch) fluted flan dish with
the pastry and bake blind (see page 6).

Heat the oil and sweat the onion in it until
transparent. Add some courgettes to the
pan. Cook for 10–15 minutes. Cook in
batches and keep hot.

Lift the courgettes and onion out of the
oil with a slotted spoon and put neatly into
the warm flan case. Season. Beat together
the eggs and milk. Pour carefully into the
flan case and sprinkle the cheese over the
top. Cook for 20–30 minutes until set and
browned. Serve hot or cold.

BUTTERSCOTCH FLAN

Serves 4–6

*175 g (6 oz) pâte sucrée (see
   page 22)
100 g (4 oz) soft dark brown sugar
50 g (2 oz) cornflour
425 ml (¾ pint) milk
2 egg yolks
25 g (1 oz) butter
2 tsp honey
150 ml (¼ pint) whipping cream
25 g (1 oz) flaked almonds,
   browned*

Heat the oven to 200°C (400°F) mark 6.
Line an 18-cm (7-inch) fluted flan case with
the pastry. Bake blind (see page 6).

Put the sugar, cornflour (blended with a
little of the milk) and the rest of the milk
into a pan. Cook until the mixture thickens,
stirring all the time. Remove from the heat.
Beat the egg yolks and stir in, followed by
the butter and honey. Cook for a further
few minutes. Leave to cool. When cold
pour into the cooked pastry case.

Decorate with the firmly whipped cream,
either piped or swirled on to the top of the
filling. Scatter toasted almond flakes over
the cream.

To brown the nuts – just put them into a
non-stick frying pan and toss them over a
gentle heat. They brown readily because of
the oil in them. Alternatively toast under a
moderate grill.

DEVONSHIRE FLAN

Serves 4–6

*175 g (6 oz) pâte sucrée (see
   page 22)
450 g (1 lb) cooking apples
2 cloves
75 g (3 oz) caster sugar
1 or 2 eating apples
lemon juice
apricot glaze (see page 23)*

Heat the oven to 200°C (400°F) mark 6.
Line a 20-cm (8-inch) flan dish with the
pastry. Bake blind (see page 6).

Chop the cooking apples roughly.
Simmer in very little water with the cloves
until tender. Remove the cloves and rub the
apples through a sieve. Sweeten to taste
with the sugar.

Spoon the purée into the cooked pastry
case. Quarter, core, but do not peel, the
eating apples. Cut into thin slices and dip in
lemon juice to keep them white. Arrange
decoratively on top of the puréed apple.
Pour or brush warm apricot glaze over the
fruit. Serve with lots of clotted cream.

GREEK HONEY PIE

Serves 4–6
225 g (8 oz) pâte frolle (see page 22)
100 g (4 oz) cottage cheese
100 g (4 oz) honey
50 g (2 oz) ground almonds
2 eggs, beaten
milk
a little caster sugar

Heat the oven to 200°C (400°F) mark 6 with a baking sheet in the oven. Roll out the pastry and cut two circles to fit a 20-cm (8-inch) ovenproof plate – an enamel one if possible. Line the plate with a circle of pastry.

Mix together the cheese, honey and ground almonds. Add the eggs and stir thoroughly. Put the mixture onto the pastry on the plate. Brush the edge with milk and cover with the second pastry circle. Press the edges firmly together. Decorate with fluting or the tip of a spoon.

Brush with milk and dust lightly with caster sugar. Stand on the hot baking sheet to ensure the bottom is well cooked and cook for 30–40 minutes.

NORSKA LINSER

Makes 12–14

225 g (8 oz) lemon pastry, chilled
  (see page 23)
icing sugar

Custard
175 ml (6 fl oz) single cream
2 egg yolks
1 tbsp sugar
2 tsp cornflour
grated rind and juice of 1 lemon

Heat the oven to 200°C (400°F) mark 6. Roll out the pastry on a board lightly dredged with cornflour. Using a heart-shaped cutter approximately 7.5 x 5 cm (3 x 2 inches), cut out 24 or so pastry hearts. Turn them over and leave to relax.

For the custard: mix all the remaining ingredients together with the grated rind of the lemon. Beat well and cook in the top of a double saucepan until thick. The cornflour will stop the cream from separating, but do not let it boil. Cool.

Put half the hearts on to a baking sheet lined with non-stick baking paper. Spoon a little thick custard on to the centre of each. Brush the edges with water and carefully put on the other hearts to form the lids. Press down gently. Cook for 20 minutes.

Transfer to a wire rack. When cool, dust sparingly with sieved icing sugar or, if you prefer, use the juice of the lemon with a little icing sugar for equally sparing lemon glacé icing.

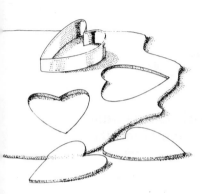

These are attractive and delicious little Scandinavian pastries, just right for engagement parties, weddings, anniversaries and christenings. In very good kitchen shops you can sometimes find trays of shallow heart-shaped tartlet tins. These obviously allow a little more filling. My heart-shaped cutter belongs to an old fashioned set of bridge biscuit cutters.

LEMON CHEESECAKE

Serves 4–6

175 g (6 oz) lemon pastry (see page 23)
2 eggs
175 g (6 oz) cottage cheese
grated rind and juice of 1 lemon
25 g (1 oz) caster sugar
2 tsp plain flour
25 g (1 oz) raisins, soaked in rum overnight

Heat the oven to 200°C (400°F) mark 6. Roll out the pastry on a board lightly dredged with cornflour. Lift the pastry on the rolling pin and use to line a greased ovenproof 18 or 20-cm (7 or 8-inch) flan case. Push it down with a little ball of the pastry and trim the edges.

Separate the eggs. Sieve the cheese. Stir the rind and juice of the lemon into the cheese. Mix the yolks and cheese together. Beat the egg whites until stiff, folding in the sugar and flour as you beat. Fold into the cheese mixture.

Spoon the filling in to the pastry case. Sprinkle the rum-soaked raisins over it: some will sink. Cook for 45 minutes until firm and lightly browned.

FLAKY PASTRY

This chapter includes many variations for using flaky pastry – both sweet and savoury – together with recipes for sauce mornay and crème pâtissière.

Flaky pastry is made by a mixture of the methods for short and puff pastry. Some fat is rubbed in, the rest flaked on to the rolled-out dough. Flaking and rolling three times produces the light, airy pastry known as 'flaky'. It is essential to have everything as cool as possible and to understand that the object is to have thin layers of fat between very thin layers of dough, entrapping air as you work. The heat expands the air, which lifts the thin dough.

FLAKY PASTRY

175 g (6 oz) margarine and lard,
    mixed
225 g (8 oz) plain flour
¼ tsp salt
150 ml (¼ pint) cold water

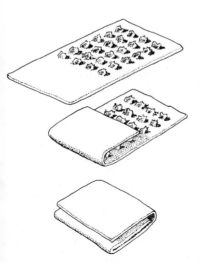

Mix the fats, divide into four and cool. Sieve the flour and salt into a basin. Rub in one part of the fat lightly with the fingertips. Add the water and mix to a soft dough. Turn out on to a board lightly dredged with cornflour and knead until smooth. This kneading is important for it distributes the ingredients evenly and strengthens the fibres of the dough. Cool for 20 minutes wrapped in greaseproof paper, foil or polythene to prevent a skin forming.

*Roll out the dough to an oblong, brushing off surplus flour. Flake one portion of fat over the upper two-thirds of the pastry to within 1 cm (½ inch) of the edge. Fold the bottom one-third up and the top one-third down. Press the edges together with the rolling pin to seal the air. Cover and leave to cool for 20 minutes.

Half turn the pastry so that the folded edge is on the right hand side. Repeat from * twice more, resting and rolling in between.

Brush off the surplus flour. Rest in a cool place until firm. The pastry can be made the day before and kept in the refrigerator.

Cook at 220°C (425°F) mark 7.

SAUCE MORNAY (CHEESE SAUCE)

25 g (1 oz) butter
25 g (1 oz) plain flour
275 ml (½ pint) milk
salt and pepper
a scrape of nutmeg
50 g (2 oz) grated cheese

Melt the butter in a pan. Stir in the flour. Beat well and cook this roux for 2 or 3 minutes, stirring all the time. Gradually add the milk, beat well and simmer for 5 minutes, stirring continuously (this cooks the flour). Season with salt and pepper and the nutmeg. Remove from the heat and stir in the grated cheese.

CRÈME PÂTISSIÈRE

1 egg
1 egg yolk
25 g (1 oz) cornflour
50 g (2 oz) caster sugar
275 ml (½ pint) milk
1 vanilla pod

Put the egg and yolk into a basin and beat together. Add the sieved cornflour and beat again. Heat the milk with the vanilla pod. Remove the pod, add the milk to the egg mixture beating all the time. Pour into a clean pan and bring slowly to the boil, stirring all the time; turn down the heat and simmer for a couple of minutes. The cornflour will stop it from curdling, but care is still needed. It will set when cold and can then be used instead of cream for slices (see page 39).

Remember the egg yolks make the creaminess and egg white does the setting, so the proportion, though fiddly, is essential.

FLAKY PASTRY
33

VERY SPECIAL RABBIT PIE

Serves 6

1 rabbit, approx. 1 kg (2¼ lb)
450 g (1 lb) flaky pastry (see
   page 31)
100-g (4-oz) can pâté de foie
225 g (8 oz) belly pork
225 g (8 oz) lean ham
salt and pepper
1 egg
150 ml (¼ pint) aspic jelly

Marinade
2 tbsp brandy
1 glass white wine
2 sprigs thyme
2 bay leaves
a pinch of ground mace
a few green peppercorns
1 onion, peeled and finely chopped

Cut the meat off the rabbit, leaving all
tendons and bone for a stock pot. Cut the
meat into large dice. Prepare the marinade.
Add the pieces of rabbit, mix thoroughly
and leave for an hour or two, turning from
time to time.

Heat the oven to 220°C (425°F) mark 7.
Roll out the pastry and leave to relax.

Dice the pâté de foie (which, of course,
could be homemade). Mince the well-
trimmed pork and ham together and season
with salt and freshly ground black pepper.
Remove the sprig of thyme and the bay
leaves from the rabbit marinade.

Cut the pastry into two circles to fit a
25-cm (10-inch) enamel plate (so much
better than an ovenproof glass one). Line
the plate with one pastry circle. Pour a little
marinade on to the mixed meats and spread
half this mixture on to the pastry. Put the
diced rabbit with the green peppercorns and
onion on top. Put the diced pâté on top of
the rabbit and cover with the rest of the
minced mixture. Pour on any remaining
marinade.

Brush the edge of the pastry with water.
Put the second pastry circle on top and
press the edges well together. Decorate with
a fork and knock up the edges. Cut a hole in
the top. Garnish with pastry leaves made
from the trimmings and brush with beaten
egg.

Cook for 20 minutes, then reduce oven
temperature to 190°C (375°F) mark 5 for a
further 50–60 minutes. Lay greaseproof
paper over the pie if it is getting too brown.
To serve cold, pour 150 ml (¼ pint) of aspic
jelly into the pie when cold and allow to set
for 2–3 hours in the refrigerator. Aspic jelly
from a packet is excellent for this purpose.

PRAWN AND ASPIC TARTLETS

Makes about 12

approx. 150 ml (¼ pint) aspic jelly
175 g (6 oz) flaky pastry (see
   page 31)
75–100 g (3–4 oz) frozen prawns
fennel or dill to garnish

Make the aspic jelly. Heat the oven to 220°C (425°F) mark 7. Roll out the pastry as thinly as possible and cut into rounds with a 5-cm (2-inch) fluted cutter to fit patty tins. Position pastry in the tins, pressing gently in with a little ball of pastry. Bake blind (see page 6). Cool on a wire rack.

Melt the prawns in warm water. Drain and pat dry. Put 1 or 2 prawns into each tartlet. Spoon the cold aspic, almost at setting point, over the prawns. Leave to set.

Garnish each tartlet with the smallest feather of fennel or dill (easy to grow).

Aspic jelly powder is excellent for this.

LEEK PIE

Serves 4–6

6 young leeks, washed and thinly
   sliced
4 rashers bacon
1 bay leaf
black pepper
water or stock
1 egg, beaten
2 tbsp top of the milk
175 g (6 oz) flaky pastry (see
   page 31)

Heat the oven to 220°C (425°F) mark 7. Rind the bacon, and cut into small strips. Put leeks and bacon with the bay leaf and black pepper into a pan. Cover with water or stock. Simmer until the liquid has almost gone. Take off the heat and cool a little. Beat the egg with the top of the milk and stir most of it into the leek mixture, retaining a little for glazing. Spoon into a shallow pie plate.

Roll the pastry out thinly, a little larger than the dish. Cut a strip for the edge of the dish. Dampen the edge and press the strip on to it. Dampen the strip, cover the pie with the pastry and press well down. Knock up the edges with the back of a knife.

Brush the pastry with the remains of the egg and milk. Make a hole in the top to let the steam out. Cook for 30 minutes until golden brown.

POACHER'S PIES

Makes about 6

350 g (12 oz) flaky pastry (see
    page 31)
homemade mustard (see page 74)
175 g (6 oz) smoked streaky bacon
100 g (4 oz) mushrooms
100 g (4 oz) pork sausagemeat
100 g (4 oz) cooked chicken or
    pheasant
1 tsp fresh thyme leaves
salt and black pepper
1 egg to glaze

Heat the oven to 220°C (425°F) mark 7. Roll out the pastry thinly and cut into 10-cm (4-inch) diameter circles; leave to relax. Spread a little mustard on half the circles, the rest being 'lids'.

Rind and trim the bacon, being careful to remove any little bits of white bone. Wipe the mushrooms. Put the bacon, mushrooms, sausagemeat, chicken or pheasant and thyme through the coarse plate of the mincer. Mix well together and season with a little salt and a generous twist or two of the black pepper mill.

Put a little of this mixture on to half the pastry circles on top of the mustard. Brush the edges with water. Put on the lids, pressing the edges together firmly. Make a small cut in the top of each and brush with beaten egg. Stand the pies on a baking sheet and cook for 15 minutes then reduce temperature to 180°C (350°F) mark 4 and continue for 30 minutes. Cover with greaseproof paper if getting too brown.

ASPARAGUS FLAN

Serves 4

175 g (6 oz) flaky pastry (see
    page 31)
225–300 g (8–10 oz) asparagus or
    a 300-g (10-oz) can asparagus
    tips
salt
275 ml (½ pint) béchamel sauce (see
    page 11)

Heat the oven to 220°C (425°F) mark 7. Line an 18-cm (7-inch) ovenproof plate or flan ring with the pastry. Bake blind (see page 6). Keep hot.

Wash the asparagus; tie loosely into a bundle. Simmer in salted water until tender. Drain and cut into 2.5-cm (1-inch) lengths, discarding any hard stalks. Keep hot. Arrange the asparagus in the pastry case, reserving a few tips. Pour the hot béchamel sauce over the asparagus and garnish with the tips. Serve at once.

SUMMER VEGETABLE FLAN

Serves 4

175 g (6 oz) flaky pastry (see
   page 31)
225 g (8 oz) or more, mixed young
   vegetables
1 tomato, peeled
1 spring onion
1 tsp chopped parsley
salt and ground black pepper
275 ml (½ pint) sauce mornay (see
   page 32)
25 g (1 oz) cheese

Heat the oven to 220°C (425°F) mark 7. Line an 18-cm (7-inch) ovenproof plate or flan case with the pastry. Bake blind (see page 6).

Prepare a mixture of young summer vegetables: sliced carrots, small broad beans, peas and diced courgettes. Cut the flesh of the tomato into small squares. Finely chop the spring onion. Simmer the vegetables in salted water until just tender. Drain. Fold in the tomato and spring onion. Season well with salt and freshly ground black pepper. Add the parsley and fold it all into the sauce mornay. Fill the flan case and sprinkle with the finely grated cheese.

Serve hot or cold. If hot, return to the oven for 15 minutes.

CREAMED SPINACH FLAN

Serves 4

175 g (6 oz) flaky pastry (see
   page 31)
350 g (12 oz) frozen spinach
salt and pepper
2 eggs
100 ml (4 fl oz) double cream
2 tbsp grated cheese
milk to glaze

Heat the oven to 220°C (425°F) mark 7. Line an 18 or 20-cm (7 or 8-inch) ovenproof plate with the pastry. Neaten the edge and prick decoratively with a fork. Bake blind (see page 6). Reduce the oven temperature to 180°C (350°F) mark 4.

Cook the spinach in the water it produces as it thaws. When tender, drain well. Season with salt and freshly ground black pepper. Beat the eggs and cream together and fold into the spinach. Fill the pastry case with the mixture. Sprinkle with grated cheese.

Brush the pastry edge with milk to glaze it. Cook for about 30 minutes until golden brown on top.

CHICKEN KOULIBIAC

Serves 6

225 g (8 oz) flaky pastry (see
  page 31)
25 g (1 oz) butter
1 small onion, peeled
50 g (2 oz) mushrooms
225 g (8 oz) cold cooked chicken,
  finely chopped
100 ml (4 fl oz) chicken stock
salt and pepper
1 hard-boiled egg
1 tsp chopped parsley
1 egg to glaze

Heat the oven to 220°C (425°F) mark 7. Roll the pastry to an oblong on a lightly-floured cloth. Trim the edges. Cool and rest.

Heat the butter in a frying pan. Finely chop the onion and mushrooms and sauté until tender. Add the chicken and moisten with the stock. Season well and simmer, stirring from time to time, until the ingredients are well combined. Cool a little.

Put half the chicken mixture down the middle of the pastry, leaving a 2.5-cm (1-inch) margin of pastry at each end. Chop the egg, mix with the parsley and put down the middle of the chicken. Cover with the rest of the chicken.

Brush the edge of the pastry with beaten egg. Bring the edges up over the chicken. Press together and then press the ends together. Using the cloth, roll the Koulibiaca on to a baking sheet lined with non-stick baking paper. Brush off the surplus flour.

Roll out the pastry trimmings, and cut into thin strips. Brush the roll with beaten egg and decorate with slanting strips of pastry. Glaze again with beaten egg. Cook for 20–30 minutes.

This is a simplified version of a Russian dish, good in a buffet, served hot or cold.

PORK EN CROÛTE

Serves 4–5

350 g (12 oz) flaky pastry (see
  page 31)
450 g (1 lb) pork pie meat
½ tsp dried sage
50 g (2 oz) raisins
salt and black pepper
1 egg, beaten

Heat the oven to 220°C (425°F) mark 7. Roll out the pastry to an oblong and trim the edges. Check the pork over, removing any gristly bits, then mince it coarsely. Add the sage, raisins, seasoning and most of the egg bind the mixture together. Keep the remaining egg for glazing.

Shape the meat into a roll down the centre of the pastry. Brush one edge with water. Fold lightly over and press the edges and ends together. Place on baking paper o a baking sheet, joined side downwards. Make a pattern with a fork on the ends. Decorate with a few pastry leaves made from the trimmings around a small slit on the top. Brush with the remaining beaten egg. Cook for 30–40 minutes until golden brown.

LANCASHIRE TURNOVER

Serves 4–6

225 g (8 oz) flaky pastry (see
  page 31)
4 shallots
50 g (2 oz) butter
2 Cox's apples
225 g (8 oz) Lancashire cheese
salt and pepper
1 egg to glaze

Heat the oven to 220°C (425°F) mark 7. Roll out the pastry to an oblong and trim the edges. Simmer the shallots in the butter until transparent. Peel, core and slice the apples thinly. Turn over a time or two in the butter with the onions.

Grate the cheese over the top half of the pastry oblong, to within 2.5 cm (1 inch) of the edge. Spread the onion and apple mixture evenly over the cheese. Brush the top edges with water. Fold the bottom half up and press the edges together firmly. Decorate with a fork or knock up (see page

Cut two or three diagonal slits across the top of the pastry and brush with egg yolk. Cook for 20–30 minutes until well risen and golden brown.

CREAM SLICES

Makes 8

225 g (8 oz) flaky pastry (see
  page 31)
175 ml (6 fl oz) whipping cream
175 g (6 oz) raspberry jam
50–75 g (2–3 oz) icing sugar
a little milk

Heat the oven to 220°C (425°F) mark 7. Roll the pastry to a 30-cm (12-inch) square; trim the edges. Cut into three 10-cm (4-inch) strips. Put on baking paper on a baking sheet. Prick with a fork and leave to rest for 20 minutes. Cook for 10–12 minutes. Cool on a wire rack.

Whip the cream until stiff. With a very sharp, pointed knife cut each strip of cooked pastry into 4-cm (1½-inch) slices. Spread one slice with raspberry jam, cover with cream. Put the next slice on top, cover with jam and cream. Turn the third slice upside down and press gently on top of the slices. Make eight cream slices in this way.

Cover the top of each slice with glacé icing made from icing sugar and a little milk, letting it spread from the middle to the edge.

Some recipes suggest making the pastries up with the three larger strips, and then cutting into slices. This needs a great deal more care.

Ice some pastries with white and some with pink glacé icing to make a charming dish of pastries.

Crème pâtissière (see page 32) is also used for these slices. They are then called Vanilla Slices.

FRUIT BORDER TART

Serves 6–8

225 g (8 oz) flaky pastry (see
  page 31)
1 egg
75 g (3 oz) strawberry jam
450 g (1 lb) or more of strawberries
100 g (4 oz) caster sugar

Heat the oven to 220°C (425°F) mark 7. Roll the pastry out to a rectangle. Trim the edges. Cut a 2.5-cm (1-inch) strip from each side. Put the rectangle of pastry on to a damp baking sheet and prick all over with a fork. Brush the edges with beaten egg. Put the pastry strips, trimming to fit, on the edges of the rectangle, just inside so they don't slip off when cooking. Leave to relax for 20 minutes.

Brush the top of the pastry strips with beaten egg. Cook for 20 minutes and then cool on a wire rack.

Sieve the jam, warm it and brush the bottom of the tart with it. Hull the strawberries. Sit them on the jam, pointed end uppermost. Dissolve the sugar in 175 ml (6 fl oz) water. Boil without stirring until syrupy and just beginning to colour. Spoon over the strawberries. Serve cold with cream.

The empty case freezes perfectly. Any fruit can be used for this simple tart.

FRENCH APPLE TART

Serves 6–8

225 g (8 oz) flaky pastry (see
  page 31)
6 apples
100 g (4 oz) granulated sugar
225 ml (8 fl oz) water
1 or 2 cloves
bramble jelly
3 eggs, separated
50 g (2 oz) caster sugar
50 g (2 oz) ground almonds

Heat the oven to 220°C (425°F) mark 7. Roll out the pastry and use to line a 23-cm (9-inch) fluted ovenproof flan dish. Bake blind (see page 6). Reduce the oven temperature to 200°C (400°F) mark 6.

Peel, core and slice the apples thinly. Poach these gently in a syrup made from 100 g (4 oz) granulated sugar dissolved in 225 ml (8 fl oz) water with one or two cloves. Melt every grain before bringing the sugary water to the boil. Simmer until getting thick. When just tender, remove the apple slices from the syrup with a slotted spoon. Arrange in the pastry case. Melt the bramble jelly and spoon it over the apples.

Whip the egg whites stiffly. Whip the yolks with the caster sugar until really fluffy. Fold the whipped whites with the ground almonds into the egg yolks. Spoon on to the bramble jelly. Dust with a little caster sugar. Cook for 20–30 minutes, until honey coloured and sparkly on top.

The spare syrup will keep, if put in a jam jar with a tightly-fitting lid, until the next time you need it.

ALLUMETTES

Makes 15–20

225 g (8 oz) flaky pastry (see page 31)
175 g (6 oz) icing sugar
1 egg white
50 g (2 oz) flaked almonds

Heat the oven to 220°C (425°F) mark 7. Roll out the pastry to an oblong 25 x 15 cm (10 x 6 inches). Trim, cut in half lengthways and leave to rest for 20 minutes.

Make the royal icing: sieve the icing sugar into a basin. Put the egg white into another. Add the sieved icing sugar a spoonful at a time, beating well after each addition. Use all the sugar to obtain a firm smooth icing.

Cut the pastry into strips approximately 7.5 x 2.5 cm (3 x 1 inch). Put on to baking paper on a baking sheet. Cover each strip with royal icing, starting from the middle so that it spreads slowly outwards. Sprinkle flaked almonds over the icing. Cook for 15–20 minutes then cool on a wire rack.

Allumettes give a lift to ordinary bought ice cream and can make a dinner party dessert more interesting.

GÂTEAU ST. GEORGES

Serves 4–5

175 g (6 oz) flaky pastry (see
    page 31)
175 g (6 oz) good dark chocolate
100 g (4 oz) butter
2 eggs, separated
50 g (2 oz) caster sugar

Heat the oven to 220°C (425°F) mark 7. Roll out the pastry and use to line an 18-cm (7-inch) ovenproof flan dish. Bake blind (see page 6). Reduce the oven temperature to 180°C (350°F) mark 4.

Melt the chocolate in a basin over hot water or in a microwave. Remove from the heat and cool a little. Stir in the butter a little at a time. Beat the egg yolks and stir them into the chocolate. Mix well. Pour into the pastry case and leave until cold.

Whisk the egg whites stiffly. Fold in the caster sugar. Spoon the meringue on to the chocolate and swirl with a fork. Cook the meringue for 15 minutes. It will be marshmallowy inside, not set like a meringue shell.

Butter, not margarine and a very good chocolate are essential for this dessert.

DEVONSHIRE TURNOVERS

Makes 6

225 g (8 oz) flaky pastry (see
    page 31)
1 egg white
100 g (4 oz) strawberry jam
caster sugar

Heat the oven to 220°C (425°F) mark 7. Roll the pastry into an oblong. Trim the edges and cut into six 10-cm (4-inch) squares. Brush half way round the squares with beaten egg white. Put a spoonful of homemade strawberry jam on each. Fold over into a triangle. Press firmly just inside the edge to seal. Place on a baking sheet. Knock up the edges and put in a cool place to rest for 20 minutes.

Brush the turnovers with beaten egg white and sprinkle with caster sugar. This gives a sparkly finish. Cook for 20 minutes, then cool on a wire rack. Serve with lots of clotted cream.

NORMANDY CHERRY AND APPLE TART

Serves 8

225 g (8 oz) flaky pastry, made with
*   butter (see page 31)*
175 g (6 oz) granulated sugar
350 ml (12 fl oz) water
700 g (1½ lb) apples
50 g (2 oz) sugar
450 g (1 lb) cherries
2 tsp Calvados
2 tsp kirsch

Heat the oven to 220°C (425°F) mark 7. Roll out the pastry and use to line a 20-cm (8-inch) fluted ovenproof pastry dish. Bake blind (see page 6). At the same time cook two 2.5-cm (1-inch) strips of pastry which will fit all the way across the pastry case. They will be used to mark the tart into quarters.

Make a sugar syrup with the granulated sugar and the water over a gentle heat until dissolved. Then boil without stirring until syrupy but not coloured. Put aside.

Peel, core and cut up half the apples. Simmer them in as little water as possible with the caster sugar, to make an apple purée. Pour half the sugar syrup into a clean pan (a cheap frying pan kept for this purpose is useful). Peel, core and slice the rest of the apples thinly. Poach them very gently in the sugar syrup until just tender. Lift them out to drain. Reserve the syrup. Wipe and stone the cherries. Poach them in the other half of the syrup for just a minute or two. Drain. Reserve this syrup.

Put the pastry strips across the tart – tuck them in on to the bottom. Fill the two opposite quarters with puréed apple. Arrange apple slices decoratively on it, overlapping a little. Arrange the cherries in the other two quarters. Bring the apple syrup to the boil, reduce a little. Stir in the Calvados and spoon over the apples. Do the same with the cherry syrup, add the kirsch and spoon over the cherries. Leave to set. Serve with thick cream handed separately.

The syrups can be combined and used again. You can see these tarts in all the pâtisseries in Normandy. They won't taste nearly as good as your own homemade tart.

CREAM HORNS

Makes 8

225 g (8 oz) flaky pastry (see
  page 31)
1 egg
milk
150 ml (¼ pint) whipping cream
50 g (2 oz) raspberry jam

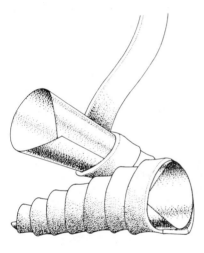

Prepare the cream horn tins – brush them
with melted white fat, not necessarily lard,
but butter and margarine are inclined to
stick. Put in a cool place. Heat the oven to
220°C (425°F) mark 7.

Roll out the pastry to a rectangle about
20 x 25 cm (8 x 10 inches). Cut into strips
2.5 x 25 cm (1 x 10 inches). Brush one edge
of each strip with lightly beaten egg. Roll on
to the outside surface of the horn tins
starting at the pointed end and ensure that
the pastry does not come over the open end
of the tin. Overlap each new turn of pastry.
Press gently on to baking paper on a baking
sheet, the tail of the pastry underneath.
Brush with milk. Cook for 15–20 minutes.

Take the horns gently off the baking
paper. Cool on a wire rack and, as they cool,
remove the tins from the pastry.

Whip the cream until stiff. Put a little
raspberry jam into the tip of the pastry
horn (a coffee spoon is handy.) Fill with
cream.

ECCLES CAKES

Makes 8

225 g (8 oz) flaky pastry (see
  page 31)
50 g (2 oz) butter
100 g (4 oz) currants
50 g (2 oz) chopped peel
50 g (2 oz) brown sugar
1 egg white
caster sugar

Heat the oven to 220°C (425°F) mark 7. Roll
out the pastry to a rectangle 30 x 15 cm
(12 x 6 inches). Trim the edges, cut into
two pieces, 30 x 7.5 cm (12 x 3 inches)
then cut each half into four 7.5 cm (3 inch)
squares. Leave to relax.

Melt the butter in a pan. Add the
currants, peel and sugar. Put a little of the
mixture into the centre of each square.
Damp the edges and draw up like a little
purse. Turn over and roll gently into a
round, about 7.5 cm (3 inches) across.

Place on baking paper on a baking sheet. Slash the top with a knife to make a criss-cross pattern. Rest for 20 minutes. Cook for 15 minutes. Brush with egg white, sprinkle with caster sugar and return to the oven for a further 5 minutes. Cool on a wire rack.

Both Banbury and Eccles Cakes need the resting after rolling to their characteristic shapes. It helps to keep that particular shape whilst these cakes are being cooked.

BANBURY CAKES

Makes 6

25 g (8 oz) flaky pastry (see page 31)
5 g (1 oz) butter
tbsp plain flour
00 g (4 oz) currants
5 g (1 oz) mixed peel
0 g (2 oz) soft brown sugar
scrape or two of nutmeg
tbsp milk
egg white to glaze
aster sugar

Heat the oven to 220°C (425°F) mark 7. Roll out the pastry to a rectangle 30 x 15 cm (12 x 6 inches). Leave to relax. Melt the butter in a pan, stir in the flour and cook for a minute or two, stirring all the time. Remove from the heat. Stir in the fruit, brown sugar, spice and milk. Leave to cool.

Trim the edges of the pastry. Cut in half lengthways. Cut each half into three equal pieces. Put a little of the mixture on to each piece. Damp the edges and draw them up into a little purse. Turn them over. Roll in one direction to an oval about 12.5 x 9 cm (5 x 3½ inches). Put on to baking paper on a baking sheet and rest for 20 minutes.

Make three cuts with a sharp knife across the top of each oval. Cook for 15 minutes then brush lightly with beaten egg white and dust with caster sugar. Bake a further 5 minutes. Cool on a wire rack.

PUFF AND ROUGH PUFF PASTRY

In addition to sweet and savoury puff and rough puff pastry dishes, this chapter includes a recipe for Cumberland sauce.

Puff and Rough Puff Pastries take time to make because of the rolling and folding processes necessary to entrap the air between the layers of pastry; this gives the traditional flaked texture. However, the effort is well worthwhile and once the simple art has been mastered, it will encourage further use of these mouthwatering pastries. Puff is the richer of the two, while rough puff is the easier and quicker to make (hence the name).

Both pastries freeze extremely well, so it is possible to make up a double quantity and store the excess, wrapped in thick polythene or foil in the freezer, for up to 3 months. They will also keep in the refrigerator for 3–4 days if closely wrapped.

Keep everything as cool as possible, use the fingertips and roll out with short, sharp definite strokes (in one direction only); this which prevents over-stretching or pulling out of shape, thus giving every reason for the pastry *not* to shrink during cooking.

It is better to dust the pastry board with cornflour rather than flour. It is very light and silky and does not unbalance the recipe by adding more flour to it.

Left-over scraps of pastry can also be frozen. Lay them one on top of the other; this keeps the fibres the right way and the pastry will roll out properly and cook better than if you scrump the scraps up into a ball. Tiny snippets of left-over unsweetened pastry make delicious little mouthfuls if dropped into boiling soup or a stew for a few minutes.

It is useful to know just how much pastry you need when preparing your own recipes. The following is a rough guide: 350 g (12 oz) puff, rough puff or flaky pastry covers a 1-litre (2-pint) pie dish or a 23-cm (9-inch) pie plate. It makes eighteen 6.5-cm (2½-inch) tartlets, or 12 cream horns.

Although it is time-consuming to make and needs
practice to overcome the hazards of inexperience,
homemade puff pastry has an incomparable taste
and texture. A lovely skill to master.

Frozen puff pastry can be bought everywhere and
is good as well as useful. All the following recipes
can be made with frozen or homemade puff or
rough puff. They are interchangeable with flaky
pastry too.

PUFF PASTRY

175 g (6 oz) plain flour
pinch of salt
175 g (6 oz) butter
approx. 150 ml (¼ pint) ice-cold
*   water*

Sieve the flour and salt together in a bowl.
Rub in a walnut of butter. Add sufficient
water to mix to a firm dough. Roll out to an
oblong about 1 cm (½ inch) thick. The
butter should be firm; not soft, not hard.

Put the butter, shaped into an oblong pat
on to the lower half of the dough. Fold the
top half down. Press the edges together.
Leave to cool for 15–20 minutes. With the
sealed ends towards you, roll lightly but
firmly away from you into the original
oblong. Do not 'push'. (Roll out on a
surface lightly dredged with cornflour. It is
smooth and light and does not clog up the
works.)

Fold the pastry into three; bottom third
upwards and top third downwards. Turn
the open end towards you. Roll out again to
an oblong. Repeat folding and rolling
process twice more. Fold in three again and
leave to rest and relax before using.

This pastry freezes well and can also be
kept in the refrigerator wrapped in a
dampish cloth for two or three days. Puff
pastry is cooked at 220–230°C (425–450°F)
mark 7–8.

ROUGH PUFF PASTRY

175 g (6 oz) plain flour
pinch of salt
150 g (5 oz) butter
approx 150 ml (¼ pint) iced water

Sieve the flour and salt into a bowl. Cut the butter into walnut-sized pieces. Mix these pieces into the flour – do not rub in. Add sufficient water to mix to a firm dough. Leave to rest in a cool place for 15 minutes.

Turn on to a surface lightly dredged with cornflour. Press the dough lightly together. Roll lightly and evenly into a strip about ½–1 cm (¼–½ inch) thick. Fold into three as for puff pastry and press the edges lightly together to entrap air. Give the pastry a half-turn. Roll out to an oblong again, fold in three and give a half-turn. Repeat the rolling and folding process three times. Leave to cool and relax before using. Cook as for puff pastry at 220–230°C (425–450°F) mark 7–8.

CUMBERLAND SAUCE

4 tbsp redcurrant jelly
2 sugar lumps
1 orange
1 lemon
2 glasses port
1 tsp arrowroot

Put the jelly in a pan. Take the zest off the orange with the sugar lumps. Add to the pan with the orange juice, the finely grated rind and juice of the lemon. Simmer gently for a few minutes. Strain and return to the pan. Add the port, bring to the boil and stir in the arrowroot, slaked with a tablespoon of water. This is best made the day before it is needed.

SALMON AND MUSHROOM SLICE

Serves 4–6

225 g (8 oz) puff pastry (see page 48)
50 g (2 oz) butter
1 onion, peeled
25 g (1 oz) plain flour
150 ml (¼ pint) milk
salt and pepper
nutmeg
200 g (7 oz) cooked fresh salmon, flaked or 200-g (7-oz) can salmon, drained
75 g (3 oz) mushrooms
1 egg to glaze
fennel or dill to garnish

Heat the oven to 220°C (425°F) mark 7. Roll out the pastry to an oblong about 45 x 15 cm (18 x 6 inches) – this will be thin. Trim the edges and cut in half. Put one half on baking paper on a baking sheet. Leave pastry to relax.

Melt the butter and fry the finely chopped onion until tender but not brown. Stir in the flour. Mix well. Add the milk by degrees, stirring all the time. Bring to the boil and cook for a minute. Season with salt, freshly ground black pepper and the merest scrap of nutmeg. Mix in the flaked fish, being very careful about removing all bones.

Put half of the salmon mixture on to the pastry on the baking sheet leaving a 2.5-cm (1-inch) gap around the edges. Wipe the mushrooms, slice them thinly and lay over the salmon. Then cover with the other half of the salmon mix. Brush the pastry edges with beaten egg. Give the second piece of pastry a light roll to make it a little larger than the bottom piece. Fold it in half lengthways. With a sharp knife make four slanting cuts through the fold. Still folded, put it on to one half of the slice. Open it out to cover the other half. Press the edges together. Knock them up and brush the top with beaten egg. Cook for 20–30 minutes.

Garnish with the smallest feather or two of dill or fennel. Both can be easily grown in the garden.

CHILLI WHIRLS

Makes about 30

50 g (12 oz) puff pastry (see
  page 48)
50 g (12 oz) minced beef
5 g (3 oz) red and green peppers,
  mixed
small onion, peeled
tsp mild chilli powder (not
  powdered chilli)
tbsp homemade tomato sauce (see
  page 63) or bought
alt
tsp cornflour
tbsp water
egg to glaze
75 g (3 oz) cheese

Heat the oven to 220°C (425°F) mark 7. Roll
out the pastry to a 30-cm (12-inch) square.
Cut in half and leave to relax.

Fry the beef, finely chopped peppers and
onion together in a pan until brown. Stir in
the chilli powder, tomato sauce, salt and
cornflour blended in the water. Cook for a
few minutes, stirring well together. Cool.

Trim the edges of the pastry. Spread the
mince over each piece to within 2.5 cm
(1 inch) of the edge. Brush one edge of each
with beaten egg. Roll up towards the
egg-washed edges to form two rolls with the
join underneath. Lift each roll on to a
baking sheet lined with baking paper.
Brush with beaten egg. Cut each roll into 15
slices, putting each piece flat on the baking
paper as you cut it. (It *does* work out all
right.)

Sprinkle grated cheese on top of each
whirl. Cook for about 20 minutes until
golden and puffed up; watch them
carefully.

All the ingredients for these can be in your
freezer or store cupboard and they are a
change from the everlasting burger. They
freeze perfectly. Re-heat to crisp up.

When buying mince, think carefully.
'Minced beef' can be all sorts of beef
minced and may be fatty and even have bits
of gristle in it. Minced beef steak may be
called 'minced chuck steak' and will be
tender and lean, though more expensive. It
is worth it every time to buy
home-produced mince, of whatever quality,
from a reputable source.

STEAK AND KIDNEY PIE

Serves 4

700 g (1½ lb) braising steak
175 g (6 oz) ox kidney
25 g (1 oz) plain flour
salt and pepper
25 g (1 oz) dripping
1 onion, peeled and chopped
275 ml (½ pint) stock or water
1½ tsp homemade mustard (see page 74)
225 g (8 oz) puff pastry (see page 48)
1 egg to glaze

Cut the steak and kidney into cubes, trimming excess fat, gristle and tubes away. Season the flour and toss the meat in it. Heat the dripping and fry the onion until brown. Add the meat and brown. Stir in the stock and mustard. Cover the pan and simmer slowly for 1½ hours then leave to cool.

Heat the oven to 230°C (450°F) mark 8. Roll out the pastry to fit the top of a 1-litre (1¾-pint) oval or rectangular pie dish. Leave to relax.

Spoon the meat into the dish. From the pastry trimmings roll out a 2.5-cm (1-inch) strip. Damp the edges of the dish, put on the strip; moisten it and carefully position the lid over the meat. Press the edges firmly together. Decorate the edge with the prongs of a fork. Knock up the edges (see page 7). Cut out a few leaves and a rose and put around the slit cut in the top of the pie to let out the steam. Brush with beaten egg.

Cook for 30 minutes, covering with greaseproof paper if it starts getting too brown.

CURRIED CHICKEN PIE

Serves 4–6

350 g (12 oz) rough puff pastry (see page 49)
275 ml (½ pint) béchamel sauce (see page 11)
1 tsp curry paste, or more to taste
225 g (8 oz) cold cooked chicken, diced
225 g (8 oz) cold cooked ham, diced
salt and pepper

Heat the oven to 220°C (425°F) mark 7. Roll the pastry out to a circle to fit a 23-cm (9-inch) ovenproof plate. Cut a 2.5-cm (1-inch) strip from around the edge. Leave to relax.

Make a béchamel sauce and add the curry paste according to your taste. Stir in the diced meats. It is important to have no skin or tendon, no gristly bits and not too much ham fat. Season well. Stir in the lemon

½ tsp lemon juice
milk to glaze

juice. Spoon the mixture on to the plate. Damp the rim of the plate. Fit on the pastry strip and damp the strip. Lift the pastry over a rolling pin, and use to cover the meat. Press the edges together. Scallop the edges with a spoon and knock them up with the back of a knife (see page 7).

Brush the pie with milk to glaze and cook for about 30–40 minutes until well risen and golden brown.

This is a good dish for after Christmas, using turkey and ham or tongue. A well flavoured béchamel is the secret of the dish.

FENNEL SAVOURY PUFFS

Serves 2

175 g (6 oz) puff pastry (see
  page 48)
2 fennel bulbs
salt and pepper
25 g (1 oz) butter
25 g (1 oz) plain flour
275 ml (½ pint) chicken stock
4 tbsp milk
2 tbsp tomato purée
75 g (3 oz) cooked lean ham

Roll out the pastry. Cut two circles to cover individual ovenproof bowls, about 12.5 cm (5 inches) across. Leave to relax. Heat the oven to 220°C (425°F) mark 7.

Wash the fennel. Trim the tops and slice off the base. (Use the trimmings for the stock pot.) Cut into thick slices and cook in boiling salted water for 15 minutes. Make a quick sauce by putting the butter, flour, stock and milk into a saucepan and whisking over a low heat until thick and creamy. Stir in the tomato purée and season well. Chop the ham finely and stir into the sauce.

Divide the fennel between the dishes, pour the sauce over the fennel and leave to cool a little. Put the pastry circles lightly on top of the fennel in the dishes. Brush with milk. Cook for 20 minutes or until puffed and golden brown. The pastry circles sit, crisp and light, on top of the savoury fennel mixture.

LAPIN AUX PRUNEAUX

Serves 6

1 rabbit, approx. 1 kg (2¼ lb)
275 ml (½ pint) red wine
10 prunes
1 small onion
sprig of thyme
350 g (12 oz) puff pastry (see
  page 48)
50 g (2 oz) dripping
25 g (1 oz) plain flour
½ tsp green peppercorns
salt and pepper
1 egg to glaze
150 ml (¼ pint) stock

Cut the flesh off the rabbit, discarding tendons and bones – put these in the stock pot. Marinate the rabbit flesh in the wine overnight with the stoned prunes, finely chopped onion and thyme.

Roll out the pastry to a circle to cover a 23-cm (9-inch) fluted ovenproof dish. Leave to relax. Heat the oven to 230°C (450°F) mark 8.

Lift the rabbit, prunes and onion out of the marinade. Drain and fry in the dripping until the rabbit is browned. Stir in the flour, add a little marinade, stir well and add further marinade to make a thick gravy. Stir in the green peppercorns. Season to taste. Spoon the rabbit mixture into the dish and leave to cool.

Brush the fluted rim of the dish with beaten egg. Lift the pastry on a rolling pin and cover the dish. Cut neatly around the fluting with a very sharp little knife.

Brush the pastry with beaten egg. Make a hole in the centre to the let the steam out. Cook until risen and golden brown for about 20–30 minutes. Cover the pastry with greaseproof paper if it starts getting too brown. Serve hot. Make a gravy with the remaining stock and the marinade, reduced to 150 ml (¼ pint) by boiling.

This dish is from Picardy.

LAMB EN CROÛTE

Serves 6

350 g (12 oz) puff pastry (see
   page 48)
1.4 kg (3 lb) leg of lamb
4 lamb's kidneys
50 g (2 oz) butter
100 g (4 oz) button mushrooms
100 g (4 oz) fresh brown
   breadcrumbs
¼ tsp powdered rosemary
salt and freshly ground black pepper
1 egg to glaze

Roll out the pastry to a rectangle about
35 x 40 cm (14 x 16 inches). Trim, release
from the board and leave to relax in a cool
place. Heat the oven to 190°C (375°F)
mark 5.

Cut away most of the fat from the lamb,
leaving just a thin layer. Bone the lamb
using a sharp knife or ask your butcher to
do so. Feel with your fingers to make sure
no little bits of bone have been left behind.
Remove the skins and cores from the
kidneys. Dice them and sauté in the butter.
Slice the mushrooms and add them to the
pan with the breadcrumbs and rosemary.
Season well and cook for a few minutes
longer. Cool.

Stuff the lamb with the kidney mixture.
Press the joint back into a reasonable shape.
Tie firmly with string. Put the lamb, open
end down, on to crumpled foil in the
roasting tin. Cook for 1 hour then take out
of the oven and cool. Remove the string.
Increase the oven temperature to 230°C
(450°F) mark 8.

Put the cold lamb on to the pastry. Brush
the pastry edges with beaten egg and fold up
over the lamb to enclose it. Put this parcel
on to baking paper on a baking sheet, joins
downwards. Cut a hole in the top to let out
the steam. Brush the pastry all over with
beaten egg to which a little water has been
added. Make pastry leaves from the pastry
trimmings and arrange around the hole.
Glaze with egg.

Cook for 30 minutes or until well risen
and dark golden brown. Cover the leaves
lightly with foil if the pastry starts to get too
brown. Serve hot with Cumberland sauce
(see page 49).

GÂTEAU PITHIVIERS

Serves 4–6

*350 g (12 oz) puff pastry (see
  page 48)*
50 g (2 oz) butter
50 g (2 oz) caster sugar
50 g (2 oz) ground almonds
1 egg white to glaze
sugar to glaze

Heat the oven to 220–230°C (425–450°F) mark 7–8. Roll out the pastry and cut two 18-cm (7-inch) circles from it. Roll one out a little larger. Leave to relax.

Make the filling – a crème pithiviers: cream the butter and sugar together, add the ground almonds and egg yolk. Stir well.

Line a baking sheet with baking paper. Lift the smaller circle of pastry on to it. Roll out the trimmings. Cut a 2.5-cm (1-inch) strip from them. Brush the pastry circle edge with water and press the strip gently around it. This will stop the filling from leaking out.

Spoon the filling on to the base. Brush the strip with water. Lift the second circle on to it. Press lightly with the fingertips to seal. Decorate the edges with the tip of a spoon. Knock up with the back of a knife. Cut a hole in the top to let out the steam and with the point of a sharp knife, lightly cut the traditional cartwheel whirls on the top. Brush with beaten egg white and dust with caster sugar. Cook until honey coloured and well risen for about 30 minutes. Serve cold with cream.

APRICOT JALOUSIE

Serves 6–8

*350 g (12 oz) puff pastry (see
  page 48)*
100 g (4 oz) apricot jam
450 g (1 lb) fresh apricots
100 g (4 oz) caster sugar
275 ml (½ pint) water
1 tbsp Benedictine

Heat the oven to 220–230°C (425–450°F) mark 7–8. Roll out the pastry to a 30-cm (12-inch) square. Cut in half lengthwise. Roll one piece a little larger. Trim both. Put the smaller piece on to baking paper on a baking sheet.

Sieve the jam and spread it on this piece of pastry to within 2.5 cm (1 inch) of the edge. Cut the apricots in half, removing the

1 egg to glaze
sugar to glaze

stones. Dissolve the sugar in the water and boil for a few minutes. Gently poach the apricots in the syrup for a few minutes. Lift out with a slotted spoon. Drain and arrange attractively on the jam on the pastry. Sprinkle with Benedictine. Brush the edge with some beaten egg.

Dust the second piece of the pastry with cornflour. Fold in half lengthwise, flour side inside. With a very sharp knife make slits right through the pastry 2.5 cm (1 inch) apart. Unfold and put carefully over the apricots, pressing the edges together to seal. Decorate the edges by cutting with a knife, and knock up. Brush with beaten egg, being careful not to brush the slits together. Dust with caster sugar. Cook for 30 minutes until golden brown.

Both these traditional French pastries (gâteau pithiviers and apricot jalousie) will freeze well. Like all pastry dishes they need crisping in the oven after defrosting.

CONQUES

Makes about 30

175 g (6 oz) puff pastry (see page 48)
caster sugar

Heat the oven to 220°C (425°F) mark 7. Roll out the pastry as thin as possible. Cut out small circles with a 4-cm (1½-inch) cutter.

Sprinkle the board with caster sugar. Elongate each little circle on the sugar with the rolling pin. Leave to relax. Place on a baking sheet lined with non-stick baking paper. Cook for about 10 minutes (but watch them). Cool on wire racks. Store in an airtight tin. Serve with ices or fools. They may need crisping before use.

BANANA TURNOVERS

Makes 4

175 g (6 oz) puff pastry (see
    page 48)
2 tbsp jam
4 bananas
1 lemon
50 g (2 oz) soft brown sugar
1 egg to glaze
25 g (1 oz) flaked almonds

Heat the oven to 220–230°C (425–450°F) mark 7–8. Roll out the pastry and use to cut four circles about 15 cm (6 inches) across. Leave to relax for 20 minutes. Then brush each circle with jam to within 1 cm (½ inch) of the edge.

Mash the bananas with the grated rind and juice of the lemon and the sugar. Spoon into the centres of the pastry circles. Brush around half the edge of each circle with beaten egg. Fold over, press together and flute the edges, and knock them up. Stand on a baking sheet and brush the turnovers with beaten egg.

Cook for 15–20 minutes until starting to brown. Sprinkle with flaked almonds and return to the oven for a further 5 minutes. Serve hot or cold. Rum can be added to the mashed banana.

MILLE FEUILLES

Serves 4–6

350 g (12 oz) puff pastry (see
    page 48)
450 g (1 lb) raspberries
75 g (3 oz) caster sugar
275 ml (½ pint) whipping cream
100 g (4 oz) icing sugar
a little milk

Heat the oven to 220–230°C (425–450°F) mark 7–8. Roll out the pastry thinly. Cut five 20-cm (8-inch) rounds from it, using a plate as a guide. Put the rounds on baking paper on baking sheets. Prick them to prevent them from rising too high. Cook until golden brown, about 20 minutes. Cool on wire racks.

Dust the raspberries with caster sugar. Reserve a few of the best for decoration. Whip the cream and fold in the raspberries. Put a pastry circle on to the serving plate. Cover with raspberries and cream. Put on the next circle; cover with the mixture. Continue in the same way until the last circle. Put this on top.

Make a little firm glacé icing with the icing sugar and a tablespoon or less of milk. Spoon on to the top round of pastry so that it forms a small pool. Set the reserved raspberries in it. Serve fairly soon after making.

PALMIERS

Makes about 20

350 g (12 oz) puff pastry (see page 48)
caster sugar

Heat the oven to 220°C (425°F) mark 7. Roll out the pastry to a rectangle about 35 x 25 cm (14 x 10 inches). Trim the edges. Sprinkle the pastry amply with caster sugar. If you keep one or two vanilla pods in the sugar jar, so much the better.

Fold the long sides of the pastry to meet in the middle. Fold one side on to the other so that you now have a strip about 35 x 6 cm (14 x 2½ inches). Seal the strip firmly with the rolling pin.

With a sharp knife, using a pressing rather than a sawing movement, cut slices 1–2 cm (¼–½ inch) wide. Put these on baking paper on baking sheets, widely spaced, as they will expand. Leave to relax for 20 minutes. Cook until pale gold, for about 5 or 6 minutes. Cool on wire racks.

These are sometimes sandwiched together with raspberry jam and whipped cream. This makes them rather difficult to eat and it is, anyway, gilding the lily.

SUET CRUST PASTRY

This chapter includes different kinds of
dumplings and traditional meat and fruit
puddings, all of which are made with the basic
suet crust pastry recipe.

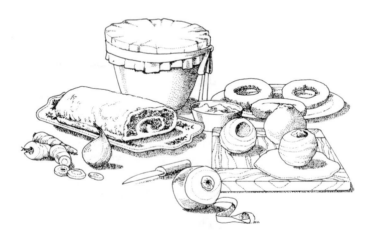

Suet crust is one of the easiest pastries to cook really well, but to achieve a light, feathery texture, care should be taken. The ingredients simply must be weighed and measured, whatever your grandmother did. The dough needs the lightest of handling and the pot must be watched to see that it does not go off the boil.

The basic recipe given below uses self-raising flour and shredded packet suet. These produce perfect results and obviously are quicker and easier than plain flour with baking powder and butcher's suet, which has to be grated.

For 'boiled' puddings (those where the basin stands in a pan of boiling water) there should be not less than 2.5 cm (1 inch) between the pudding basin and the sides of the pan. This lets the steam circulate.

The water should reach half-way up the sides of the basin. Keep an eye on the water and top up with boiling water. If the water goes off the boil the pastry will be heavy and soggy.

Boiled puddings can be cooked in a slow cooker or a microwave oven, but read the appropriate instructions before you start.

To line a basin with suet crust pastry
For a 750-ml (1½-pint) basin, you will need about 225 g (8 oz) pastry. Roll it out into a circle 5–7.5 cm (2–3 inches) larger than the top of the basin. Cut a third out in the shape of a triangle.

Grease the basin well and fit the larger piece into it on a dressmaking principle. Damp one of the edges and very slightly overlap the other. Press well together. Roll the small piece into a circle to form the lid and position it.

To cover a boiled pudding
Cover the basin with a pudding cloth, or buttered greaseproof paper, pleated and tied on, or strong kitchen foil twisted tightly under the rim. A pudding cloth can be very easily made with a stitched-on handle and string run through the hem to tie it on. It makes the putting in and getting out much easier.

Boilable plastic pudding basins with lids can be bought. Check that the lids really do clip on tightly before you buy a set. A sheet of greased greaseproof paper under the lid will make quite sure.

SUET CRUST PASTRY

225 g (8 oz) self-raising flour
½ tsp salt
100 g (4 oz) shredded suet
150 ml (¼ pint) water

Sieve the flour and salt together into a bowl. Add the suet and mix well. Pour the water on to the flour. Cut with a round-bladed knife through the mixture until all the water has been absorbed.

Turn the dough on to a floured board and knead very lightly for a minute or two. Form into a ball, cover and leave to relax for 5 minutes.

DUMPLINGS

Makes 8 small ones

100 g (4 oz) suet crust pastry (see above)
salt

Put a large pan of water on to boil. Divide the pastry into eight pieces, each about the size of a bantam's egg. With floured hands, roll each piece into a firm ball; dredge with flour. This will keep them a good shape.

Put into boiling salted water. Bring back to the boil. Cover the pan and simmer the dumplings gently for 15–20 minutes. They will break up if the water 'gallops'. Lift out with a slotted spoon.

HERB OR PARSLEY DUMPLINGS

Makes 8 small ones

100 g (4 oz) suet crust pastry (see page 62)
2 tsp chopped thyme leaves or 1 tbsp freshly chopped parsley

Make the dumplings as in the previous recipe, adding the herbs to the dry mixture. Use less if dried herbs are added.

These can be boiled in soup or served with a ragoût of beef and are delicious with boiled ham.

RICH TOMATO SAUCE

1 small onion
25 g (1 oz) butter
25 g (1 oz) lean cooked ham
450 g (1 lb) fresh ripe tomatoes
1 clove garlic
salt and pepper
1 sherry glass Marsala

Peel the onion and slice it thinly. Fry in the butter. Add the ham cut into tiny pieces. Skin and quarter the tomatoes; peel and chop the garlic. Add to the pan and season well. Simmer for 5–10 minutes, stirring with a wooden fork. Pour in the Marsala and cook for a further minute or two.

This sauce will freeze well. You could make a good deal in a tomato glut and have it tasting just as fresh at Christmas time. Cover it closely because of the garlic. Canned Italian tomatoes are useful too for this sauce if fresh ones are not readily available.

BEEFSTEAK AND KIDNEY PUDDING

Serves 4

225 g (8 oz) suet crust pastry (see
  page 62)
350 g (12 oz) chuck steak
100 g (4 oz) ox kidney
1 onion
50 g (2 oz) mushrooms
2 tbsp plain flour
salt and pepper
150 ml (¼ pint) stock

Put a pan of water on to boil. Cut the meat
into strips, trim the kidney and dice. Peel
and slice the onion. Wipe and slice the
mushrooms including the stalks.

Season the flour and toss the meat in it.
Grease a 750-ml (1½-pint) pudding basin.
Roll out the pastry and use to line the basin
(see page 61). Put the meat, kidney, onion
and mushrooms into the lined basin. Do not
pack it too tightly. Season the stock and
pour into the basin. Damp the edges of the
pastry. Roll the lid out to fit the top of the
basin, position and seal well. Cover the
basin (see page 62).

Stand the basin in the boiling water and
cover the pan. Boil steadily, not too fast, for
3–3½ hours. Keep an eye on the water level.

This traditional pudding is served in the
basin, with a linen napkin wrapped around
the outside. A small jug of boiling water is
served beside it. When the first piece of
pastry is lifted out a tablespoon or two of
boiling water is poured in, to make a little
more gravy.

Cheaper cuts of meat can be used but will
need pre-cooking. Let the meat get cold
before putting into the pudding. It will then
need 1½–2 hours' cooking.

SALMON DUMPLINGS

Makes 16

80-g (3¼-oz) can salmon
1 tsp freshly chopped parsley
225 (8 oz) suet crust pastry (see
  page 62)

Put a pan of water to boil. Drain the salmon
and remove all bones and skin. Break up the
fish with a fork and stir in the parsley.

Divide the pastry into 16 small pieces.
Flatten each piece and put a little salmon
mixture into the middle. Damp the edges

and gather up into balls. Flour well. Add to
boiling water, and cook as for plain
dumplings (see page 63).

This is an old recipe from the Severn and no
doubt the dumplings were originally made
from the odds and ends of fresh salmon.
They are delicious cooked in a spring
vegetable soup and then make a complete
meal.

BAKED MEAT ROLL

Serves 4–6

1 onion, peeled
dripping
350 g (12 oz) cooked meat, minced
1 tbsp mixed herbs
2–3 tbsp homemade tomato sauce
(see page 63) or bought
225 g (8 oz) suet crust pastry (see
page 62)

Heat the oven to 220°C (425°F) mark 7.
Chop the onion and fry in the dripping until
brown. Add the meat with the herbs and the
tomato sauce. Season well and simmer for
10 minutes. Cool.
  Roll out the pastry to an oblong. Spread
with the cooled mixture, leaving a narrow
margin. Turn in the edges to keep the filling
in. Brush with water and roll up firmly.
Place on baking paper on a baking sheet,
join side downwards. Bake for 1 hour until
golden brown and crisp. If the pastry is
getting too brown, cover it loosely with a
sheet of greaseproof paper and turn the
oven down to 200°C (400°F) mark 6.

This is a good way of using up the leftovers
of the joint.

DUTCH APPLE PUDDING

Serves 4–6

225 g (8 oz) suet crust pastry (see page 62)
450 g (1 lb) cooking apples
brown sugar
golden syrup

Heat the oven to 200–220°C (400–425°F) mark 6–7. Divide the pastry in half. Roll out one piece into a round and use to line a well greased 20-cm (8-inch) pie plate (preferably enamel). Peel, core and slice the apples. Put the slices thickly on the pastry round. Sprinkle well with sugar and damp the edge of the pastry.

Roll out the remaining pastry for a lid and cover the apple with it, pressing the edges firmly together. Brush the top of the pie generously with warmed golden syrup and sprinkle with brown sugar. Cook for 30–40 minutes until the pie is brown and the top crisp like toffee.

SUSSEX POND PUDDING

Serves 4–6

225 g (8 oz) suet crust pastry (see page 62)
50 g (2 oz) butter
50 g (2 oz) soft brown sugar
grated rind and juice of 1 lemon

Put a pan of water on to boil. Grease a 750-ml (1½-pint) pudding basin. Roll out the pastry to a thick round and use to line the basin, letting the ends fall over the edge of the basin.

Work the butter and sugar together, adding the rind and juice of the lemon. Put this mixture into the middle of the pudding. Fold the edges over the top and seal with water. Cover the basin (see page 62). Stand the basin in the boiling water and boil steadily for 2½–3 hours. Remove the basin and let stand for a minute or two. Turn out and serve plain.

PLUM JAM LAYER PUDDING

Serves 4

225 g (8 oz) suet crust pastry (see page 62) made with wholemeal self-raising flour
225 g (8 oz) homemade plum jam

Put a pan of water on to boil. Grease a 500-ml (1-pint) pudding basin. Divide the pastry into four pieces (each one slightly larger than the last). Roll the smallest piece into a round to fit the base of the basin. Cover the pastry with jam. Add another slightly larger round and cover with jam. Add a third round and cover with jam. Finish with the largest piece rolled into a round.

Cover the basin (see page 62). Stand the basin in the boiling water and boil steadily for 2 hours, topping up with boiling water as necessary.

Remove the basin and let it stand for a minute or two. The pastry will shrink a little, making it easier to turn out. Serve at once with cream or custard.

A syrup pudding can be made in the same way, using 50 g (2 oz) golden syrup with 50 g (2 oz) breadcrumbs mixed with it. Layer the pudding as for the jam one. This would be served with warm syrup.

SUET DOUGHNUTS

Makes 8 round and 8 ring doughnuts

50 g (2 oz) caster sugar
1 tsp ground cinnamon
225 g (8 oz) suet crust pastry (see page 62)
100 g (4 oz) lard or white fat or vegetable oil

Shake the sugar and cinnamon together in a paper bag. Roll out the pastry to a thickness of 1 cm (½ inch). Cut into eight 7.5-cm (3-inch) rounds. Remove the centre of the rounds using a 4-cm (1½-inch) cutter.

Heat the fat or oil in a frying pan. Gently fry the rings and the rounds for 8–10 minutes, until cooked and golden brown on both sides. Drain on absorbent kitchen paper and toss in the paper bag with the sugar. Serve at once on a hot dish.

68

GOLDEN TRIANGLES

Makes 4

100 g (4 oz) suet crust pastry (see
  page 62)
100 g (4 oz) fat or oil to fry
golden syrup or honey

Roll out the pastry into a round about 1 cm
(½ inch) thick. Cut into four triangles. Melt
the fat and shallow-fry the triangles for
8–10 minutes, turning once, until golden
brown on both sides. Serve at once with
warm golden syrup or honey.

Both these recipes are lovely for high tea on
a cold winter's night and come from old
farmhouse days.

DORSET APPLE PUDDINGS

Makes 4

50 g (2 oz) butter
50 g (2 oz) brown sugar
1 tbsp rum
4 medium eating apples
225 g (8 oz) suet crust pastry (see
  page 62)

Put a pan of water on to boil. Mix the
butter, sugar and rum together; beat until
soft. Peel and core the apples.
  Divide the pastry into four pieces. Roll
out into rounds large enough to enclose the
apples. Put an apple on each round and fill
the hole with the butter mixture. Brush the
edges of the rounds with water.
  With floured hands, enclose each apple in
its pastry, by bringing the edges to the top.
Press to seal. Loosely wrap each dumpling
in a square of good quality kitchen foil,
twisting the top firmly to seal, but leaving
room for the dumpling to expand.
  Put into boiling water and bring back to
the boil. Cover and simmer for 30–40
minutes.
  Lift the parcels out with a slotted spoon
and remove the foil. Put the dumplings on a
hot dish, sprinkle with caster sugar and
serve at once, with cream.

Eating apples cook well. They do not
collapse like Bramleys and are a good size
for these dumplings.

APPLE HAT

Serves 4–6

225 g (8 oz) suet crust pastry (see page 62)
450 g (1 lb) cooking apples
3 tbsp soft brown sugar
lemon
3 tbsp water

Put a pan of water on to boil. Grease a 750-ml (1½-pint) pudding basin. Roll out the pastry and use to line the basin (see page 61).

Peel, core and slice the apples, mix with the sugar, lemon rind and water. Damp the edges. Roll out the remaining pastry for a lid and position. Press well together.

Cover the basin (see page 62). Stand the basin in the boiling water and boil steadily for 3 hours, topping up with boiling water as necessary.

Remove the basin and let stand for 2–3 minutes. Turn out and serve with brown sugar and cream.

SPOTTED DICK

Serves 4–6

225 g (8 oz) suet crust pastry (see page 62)
100 g (4 oz) stoned raisins

Put a pan of water on to boil. Make the suet crust pastry as usual but add the raisins to the dry ingredients before adding any liquid.

Grease a 500-ml (1-pint) pudding basin. Shape the pastry into a ball and put into the basin. Cover the basin (see page 62). Stand the basin in the boiling water and boil steadily for 2 hours.

Remove the basin and let stand for a minute or two. Turn out and serve with custard.

If you like smaller spots, use currants with 50 g (2 oz) sugar in place of raisins.

HOT WATER CRUST PASTRY

Homemade pork or game pies can be both
spectacular and delicious. This chapter unveils
the secrets of how to make them in the
traditional manner – they are easier than
you think.

Hot water crust pastry is quite different from any other pastry. It has to be strong enough to stand up on its own and to hold up the weight of a pie filling which is usually, but not always, meat or game. It has to withstand long cooking in order that the closely-packed filling will be properly cooked and when it finally comes to the table, cold, it must be velvety inside and richly crisp outside.

Boiling water and lard are added to the flour, so you start with a partly-cooked dough of considerable strength. The pastry must be moulded while it is still warm. If it gets cool it will crack and be difficult to handle. However, do not try to mould it too hot. You will burn your hands and the pastry will just flop about. To keep it warm, have it in a bowl in a warm place with a cloth over it.

Pies can be raised by hand (see page 72), or moulded round a jar (see page 72), made in a loose-bottomed cake tin (see pages 72–3), or in a special hinged pie mould. Small individual pies can also be made, and are handy and delicious.

Contrary to the general idea of a raised pie as being savoury, there are one or two traditional sweet fillings. Plain wholemeal flour is recommended for some of the recipes in this chapter.

Raised pies are finished with pastry leaves and a rose or tassle fitted into a hole in the top. The filling shrinks away from the pastry as it cooks. When the pie is out of the oven and cooling, this gap is filled with a savoury jelly, poured in through the hole under the rose, which is lifted out and then put back.

Hot water crust pies are firm, crusty and the greatest fun to make. Skilfully handled they can be simply stunning centre-pieces on a cold buffet table.

A pie can be raised in three different ways:

By hand
350 g (12 oz) hot water crust pastry (see page 73)
Put one-third of the pastry aside for the lid. Pat the larger piece into a scone shape and place on a baking sheet lined with baking paper. With the thumbs inside and the fingers outside, gently shape the pastry into a hollow, then begin to raise the walls of the pie. Tie with a stiff paper cuff, and put the filling into the pie bit by bit as the walls of the pie are raised higher and higher. The filling helps hold the shape of the case.

By using a mould
450 g (1 lb) hot water crust pastry (see page 73)
The mould can be a jar or cake tin, turned upside down, and measuring 15 cm (6 inches) in diameter.

Keep the pastry warm. Cut off one-third for the lid. Roll out the rest to a circle about 30 cm (12 inches) across. Upturn the mould and dredge it heavily with flour.

Lift the pastry on a rolling pin and transfer it to the mould. Shape the pastry by pressing it firmly to the mould. Cut a double piece of greaseproof paper to go right round the pastry and cover it completely. Tie round the mould in two places. Rest the pastry in a cool place until it is firm.

Turn the mould over, stand the pastry case on a baking sheet and gently ease the mould out of the case, giving it a little twist to loosen it. Leaving the greaseproof paper still tied in a cuff around the case, put in the filling, packing it well to hold the shape of the pie. Brush the edge of the pastry with beaten egg. Roll out the remaining pastry for the lid and position it. Press the edges well together, trim and flute (see page 7) or make fine cuts with a sharp knife. When the maker is experienced, the pie can be raised using only 350 g (12 oz) pastry.

By using a cake tin
A pie can also be cooked quite easily in a conventional cake tin. Lard the tin, press non-stick baking paper around the sides and on the bottom, and lard that too. Using two-thirds of the pastry, line the tin, pushing and moulding it to the sides and base. Use the remaining one-third for the lid. Turn the pie out, once cooked, on to a folded cloth. It can then be turned up the right way before the jelly is put in. A loose-bottomed cake tin is even better than an ordinary one, and a 450-g (1-lb) loaf tin makes a handsome pork pie.

HOT WATER CRUST PASTRY

350 g (12 oz) plain flour
1 tsp salt
150 g (5 oz) lard
150 ml (¼ pint) milk and water, mixed

Sieve the flour and salt together in a bowl. Put the lard and liquid into a pan and heat gently until the lard is melted, then bring to the boil. Pour immediately on to the flour in one go and mix well with a wooden spoon.

The moment you can handle it, turn the pastry out on to a floured board. Knead it quickly and lightly. Keep the pastry warm and covered with a clean cloth. As a rough guide you will use two-thirds of the pastry for the pie and one-third for the lid.

Cook at 200°C (400°F) mark 6 unless the recipe says otherwise.

JELLIED STOCK

Makes 575 ml (1 pint)

ham bones
2 pig's trotters
1.2 litres (2 pints) water
salt
1–2 sprigs thyme

Pig's trotters with a few ham bones make a wonderful jelly. Put the ham bones with two pig's trotters into 1.2 litres (2 pints) water. Add salt and a sprig or two of thyme. Bring to the boil and simmer for several hours, reducing the jelly to 575 ml (1 pint) or less. Strain, cool and leave overnight in the refrigerator. Remove the fat when the jelly is set. Melt when needed.

SAVOURY JELLY

Makes 275 ml (½ pint)

275 ml (½ pint) stock (meat extract
*   is good for this)*
1 heaped tsp powdered gelatine
salt and pepper

This is a simpler recipe than the one for jellied stock. Put the stock and gelatine into a saucepan. Stir over a gentle heat until every grain of gelatine has disappeared. Season well. Use when the jelly is cool.

HOMEMADE MUSTARD

50 g (2 oz) each, white and black
*   mustard seed*
150 ml (¼ pint) herb vinegar
3 tbsp honey
1 tsp salt
½ tsp powdered mace

Put all the ingredients in a bowl. Leave overnight to soften the seed. Mix in a blender until thick and creamy. If too thick add a little more vinegar. Leave a proportion of the seeds whole – do not blend until there are no seeds to be seen.

Store in small jars with plastic lids. Keep airtight, or the mustard will dry out.

The flavour can be varied with different spices, different vinegars, more or less honey. The mustard is an attractive addition to the table and useful for 'devils' as well as stews and pies.

INDIVIDUAL SAUSAGE AND EGG PIES

Makes 6–8

350 g (12 oz) hot water crust pastry
  (see page 73)
350 g (12 oz) pork sausagemeat
1 egg
salt and pepper
½ tsp mixed herbs
½ tsp homemade mustard (see
  page 74)
3–4 hard-boiled eggs
1 egg or milk to glaze
savoury jelly (see page 74)

Keep the pastry warm. Heat the oven to 200°C (400°F) mark 6. Cut the pastry into six pieces. From each piece keep back one-third for the lid. Roll out the pastry and use to line 10-cm (4-inch) patty tins; roll out the lids. Mix the sausagemeat, egg, seasoning, mixed herbs and mustard together. Cut the hard-boiled eggs in half. Fill the pastry cases with the sausagemeat, putting half an egg in each.

Brush the edges of the pies with milk or beaten egg, position the lids and press well together. Cut into the edges with a sharp knife to decorate. Make a small hole in the centre of each pie. From the trimmings, make one or two leaves and a little pastry rose for each pie to go round the hole in the middle. Brush with beaten egg or milk to glaze. A pinch of salt in the beaten egg makes a very glossy glaze.

Cook for 30 minutes then reduce the temperature to 180°C (350°F) mark 4. Cover the pies with greaseproof paper and cook for a further 30 minutes.

Cool in the tins. Lift the roses off the pies and fill each with cooling jelly. Chill.

The pies should be made the day before they are needed.

To practise the handling of hot water crust pastry try these small picnic pies. I bake mine in non-stick patty tins 10 cm (4 inches) across. There are four of them in a 23-cm (9-inch) square baking tray.

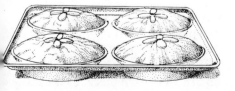

SAVOURY TOMATO PIES

Makes 4

225 g (8 oz) hot water crust pastry,
* made with 225 g (8 oz) flour,*
* 90 g (3½ oz) lard and 3½ tbsp*
* liquid (see page 73 for method)*
6 tomatoes
100 g (4 oz) green and red peppers,
* mixed*
1 onion
1 clove garlic
½ tsp chopped marjoram
1 tsp freshly chopped basil
salt and pepper
1 egg to glaze
a little stock
1 tsp powdered gelatine

Keep the pastry warm. Heat the oven to 200°C (400°F) mark 6. Skin the tomatoes and chop. Slice and de-seed the peppers. Peel and dice the onion and garlic. Reserve any juices from the vegetables. Add the herbs and season well.

Divide the pastry into four. Use to line patty tins as in the recipe for Mutton Pies, keeping one-third of each piece for the lid. Fill with the mixture and brush the edges of the pastry with beaten egg. Roll out the lids, position and press well together.

Make a hole in the top of each, flute, and decorate with a few small leaves and roses made from the trimmings. Brush with beaten egg. Cook for 30–40 minutes.

Use the reserved juice mixed with stock to make up to 150 ml (¼ pint) and dissolve the gelatine in it for a jelly. Pour into the pies when cold.

These can be made with canned tomatoes and pimentos and a pinch of dried herbs.

MUTTON PIES

Makes 6–8

350 g (12 oz) hot water crust pastry
* (see page 73)*
450 g (1 lb) lean mutton or lamb
bouquet garni
salt and pepper
2 tbsp diced carrot
1 tbsp diced onion
1 tbsp diced potato
capers
1 egg or milk to glaze
1½ tsp powdered gelatine

Keep the pastry warm. Heat the oven to 200°C (400°F) mark 6. Dice the meat. Put it into a pan with the bouquet garni, salt and pepper and barely cover with water. Simmer until just tender. Add the diced vegetables and simmer for another minute or two. Strain, reserving the stock. Put the meat and vegetables into a bowl ready for filling the pies, with just enough of the stock to moisten the mixture.

Cut the pastry into six or eight pieces. Keep one-third of each piece for the lids.

Roll out the larger pieces and use to line 10-cm (4-inch) patty tins. Fill the pastry cases with the cold meat mixture, adding one or two capers to each little pie.

Brush the edges with beaten egg, position the lids and press well together. Decorate and finish as for Individual Sausage and Egg Pies (see page 75). Cook for 20 minutes then reduce the temperature to 180°C (350°F) mark 4. Cover the pies with greaseproof paper and cook for a further 40 minutes. Cool before turning out.

Remove the bouquet garni from the stock and make the stock up to 275 ml (½ pint) with water or cider. Dissolve the gelatine in the stock. As it cools, pour into the pies through the hole in the top. Cool and chill.

These pies should be made the day before they are needed.

NDIVIDUAL PORK PIES (raised by hand)

akes 6–8

0 g (12 oz) hot water crust pastry
  (see page 73)
0 g (1 lb) lean pork
lt and pepper
  tsp mixed herbs
tbsp stock
egg to glaze
pic or savoury jelly (see page 74)

Keep the pastry warm. Heat the oven to 200°C (400°F) mark 6. Mince the meat coarsely, season well and stir in the herbs and stock.

Raise the little pies with thumb and finger straight on to a baking sheet, lined with baking paper. Work the pastry as thin as will hold the filling. Fill with the meat. Brush the edges with beaten egg. Cover with the lids. Brush all over with beaten egg. Cook for 30–40 minutes. Cover lightly with greaseproof paper and cook for another 30 minutes. When cool, fill with savoury jelly.

SMALL CHICKEN PIES (raised by hand)

Makes 6

*350 g (12 oz) hot water crust pastry
(see page 73)
350 g (12 oz) cooked chicken
salt and pepper
100 g (4 oz) mushrooms
2 rashers smoked bacon
1 egg to glaze
aspic jelly*

Keep the pastry warm. Heat the oven to 200°C (400°F) mark 6. Cut the chicken into small pieces. Be sure there are no tendons, skin or bone in it. Season well. Wipe and slice the mushrooms. Trim the bacon carefully and snip into small pieces. Sizzle the bacon in a frying pan, add the mushrooms and cook together for a minute or two. Spoon on to the chicken and mix together.

Divide the pastry into six portions and keep it warm in a covered bowl. Take one piece. Cut off one-third for the lid. Pat the larger piece into a scone shape and place on baking paper on a baking sheet. With the thumbs inside and the fingers outside gentl shape the pastry into a hollow. Raise the little pie – 4 cm (1½ inches) high and 5 cm (2 inches) across is perfectly manageable.

Fill it firmly with the chicken mixture. Neaten the top. Brush the edge with beater egg. Roll out the lid and press it on. Flute the edge. Make the rest of the pies. When all are on the baking tray, cut some small leaves and roses from the trimmings. Make a small hole in the top of each pie. Sit a rose in the hole and put one or two leaves aroun it. Brush all the pies with beaten egg – the sides as well as the top.

Cook for 40 minutes or until the pies are brown and shiny. Cool. Fill through the holes under the roses with cool aspic jelly and leave to set.

These pies should be made a day before they are needed.

RAISED GAME PIE

erves 6

50 g (1 lb) hot water crust pastry
 (see page 73)
 pheasant, approx. 1 kg (2¼ lb)
25 g (8 oz) pork pie meat
00 g (4 oz) raw gammon
ilt and pepper
 tsp mixed herbs
inch of ground mace
 egg to glaze
woury jelly or aspic (see page 74)

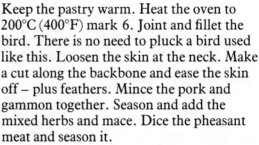

Keep the pastry warm. Heat the oven to 200°C (400°F) mark 6. Joint and fillet the bird. There is no need to pluck a bird used like this. Loosen the skin at the neck. Make a cut along the backbone and ease the skin off – plus feathers. Mince the pork and gammon together. Season and add the mixed herbs and mace. Dice the pheasant meat and season it.

Raise the pie using a mould (see page 72), or preferably for this classic pie, use a hinged 675 or 900-g (1½ or 2-lb) pie mould, well greased with lard. Ease the pastry carefully into it, and press it down using a little ball of pastry.

Put a layer of minced meat all round the inside of the pastry. Fill the centre with the pheasant meat and cover with the remaining minced meat.

Put the lid on the pie, decorate and glaze. Cook for 30 minutes. Reduce the temperature to 180°C (350°F) mark 4, cover the top with greaseproof paper and cook for a further 1½ hours. If cooked in a pie mould, give it another 30 minutes.

When cooked, take the mould off – leave the pie on the tin base. Brush all over with beaten egg and return to the oven to brown. When cold, fill with cooling savoury jelly or aspic. Tilt the pie gently to disperse the jelly inside. Chill.

Make the pie the day before it is to be eaten.

RABBIT AND PRUNE RAISED PIE

Serves 4–6

450 g (1 lb) hot water crust pastry
  (see page 73)
6 prunes
2 young rabbits, each approx.
  1 kg (2¼ lb)
salt and pepper
¼ tsp dried sage
1 onion
175 g (6 oz) raw gammon
1 tbsp chopped parsley
2 hard-boiled eggs
2 tbsp stock
1 egg to glaze
savoury jelly (see page 74)

Keep the pastry warm. Soak the prunes. Bone the rabbits and put the pieces in cold water for 1 hour. Rinse in cold water and dry. Cut the saddles and larger pieces into cubes. Season well and sprinkle with sage. Mince the small pieces of rabbit with the onion and gammon. Mix with the larger pieces. Stir in the parsley. Stone the prunes and slice the eggs. Heat the oven to 200°C (400°F) mark 6.

Raise the pie (see page 72) or prepare a cake tin or pie mould (see page 73). Fill the pie with the meat, layering it with the egg slices and adding a prune now and then. Add the stock. Cover, decorate and brush with beaten egg. Cook for 30 minutes. Reduce the temperature to 180°C (350°F) mark 4, cover with greaseproof paper, and return to the oven for a further hour. When the pie is cold, fill with savoury jelly.

This is a dish from Normandy.

VEAL AND HAM PIE

Serves 6

350 g (12 oz) hot water crust pastry
  (see page 73)
450 g (1 lb) pie veal
100 g (4 oz) raw ham
½ tsp thyme leaves
salt and pepper
1 hard-boiled egg
1 tbsp stock
1 egg to glaze
savoury jelly (see page 74)

Keep the pastry warm. Heat the oven to 200°C (400°F) mark 6. Raise the pie (see page 72). Cut the veal and ham into small pieces. Mix together with the thyme, seasonings and stock. Fill the pie case, putting the egg in the centre of the meat. Pack firmly. Cover, decorate and brush with beaten egg.

Cook for 30 minutes until the pie is beginning to brown. Reduce the temperature to 180°C (350°F) mark 4. Cover the pie loosely with greaseproof paper and cook for a further 1½ hours. Remove the paper cuff. Brush the sides with beaten egg and return to the oven for the sides to brown – about 15–20 minutes. When cold, fill the pie with cooling savoury jelly.

HARVEST PIE

Serves 6

350 g (12 oz) wholemeal hot water crust pastry (see page 73), using plain wholemeal flour instead of white
175 g (6 oz) lean smoked gammon
1 onion
450 g (1 lb) pork sausagemeat
1 egg, beaten
75 g (3 oz) mushrooms
salt and pepper
1 egg to glaze
savoury jelly (see page 74)

Keep the pastry warm. Heat the oven to 200°C (400°F) mark 6. Mince the gammon and onion together. Mix with the sausagemeat and the beaten egg. Wipe and slice the mushrooms (peel and slice if you are lucky enough to have field mushrooms). Mix them in with the sausagemeat and season to taste.

Roll out half the pastry and use to line an 18 or 20-cm (7 or 8-inch) enamel plate. Spread the filling on the pastry. Brush the edges with beaten egg. Roll out the remaining pastry for the lid. Press the edges firmly together. Cut with a knife round the edge. Make a hole in the top and brush with beaten egg. Cook for 40 minutes. Reduce the temperature to 180°C (350°F) mark 4, cover lightly with greaseproof paper and continue for a further 30–40 minutes.

This pie is good hot or cold. If to be eaten cold, fill as usual with savoury jelly. Then it is best if the pie is made the day before.

Wholemeal hot water crust is delicious. The pastry handles rather differently so try the Harvest Pie first. Then go for the duck recipe (see page 82).

CRUSTY DUCK PIE

Serves 8

350 g (12 oz) wholemeal hot water
  crust pastry (see page 73), using
  plain wholemeal flour instead of
  white
1 duck about 1.8 kg (4 lb), plucked
175 g (6 oz) raw gammon
100 g (4 oz) liver pâté
½ tsp dried sage
salt and pepper
1 egg to glaze
2 tsp powdered gelatine

Prepare the filling before making the pastry. Skin the duck. Crisp the skin in the oven: there will be nearly 275 ml (½ pint) dripping from it which can be used in another recipe. Take the meat off the duck. Keep the breast whole. Mince all the other pieces of duck with the gammon and pork. Stir in the sage and season well. Put the bones on to simmer to make a stock. Cut the duck breast into strips and dice the pâté.

Make the pastry. Heat the oven to 200°C (400°F) mark 6. Raise the pie (see page 73). A 15-cm (6-inch) cake tin is perfect for this recipe. Lard the tin well. Line with baking paper and lard that too. Take one-third of the pastry for the lid. Line the tin with the remainder of the pastry.

Fill with a layer of minced meat, then a layer of duck and pâté, until the filling is used up. Finish with a layer of minced meat. Brush the edge with beaten egg. Roll out the lid. Position and pinch the edges well together. Make a hole in the middle and cut the edges all round with a sharp knife to finish. Brush with beaten egg.

Cook for 30 minutes. Reduce the temperature to 180°C (350°F) mark 4, cover with greaseproof paper and continue for a further hour. Remove from the oven. Leave for 15 minutes then turn out on to a folded towel. Quickly turn back on to a board. Leave to cool.

Reduce the duck stock. Put 275 ml (½ pint) of it into a saucepan, season well and add the gelatine. Heat and stir until it is dissolved. Cool. Fill the pie with the jelly. Chill. Serve the next day.

This amount of pastry is just enough to line and cover the pie, using a 15-cm (6-inch) cake tin. There is none left over for leaves but the finished pie is very handsome and looks 'right'. There was just over 365 g (12½ oz) meat on the duck. (Which is why it is always served on the bone in restaurants). However, using all the ingredients, the finished pie weighed over 1.4 kg (3 lb), which is enough for 8 people.

In the 17th century England imported large quantities of 'crusty duck pies' from Picardy. The crust must have been made from brown flour – there was no other.

CHESHIRE PORK PIE

Serves 6

350 g (12 oz) hot water crust pastry
  (see page 73)
2 eating apples
3 tbsp white wine
450 g (1 lb) lean pork
1 onion
salt and pepper
pinch of dried sage
1 egg to glaze
savoury jelly (see page 74)

Keep the pastry warm. Heat the oven to 200°C (400°F) mark 6. Peel, core and chop the apples and cover them with the wine. Mince together the pork and onion. Season and add the sage and stir the apples and wine into the mixture.

Raise the pie (see page 72). Fill the case with the mixture and cover with the lid. Make some pastry leaves and a rose from the trimmings for a hole in the top. Brush with beaten egg. Cook for 30 minutes. Reduce the temperature to 180°C (350°F) mark 4, cover the top of the pie with greaseproof paper and cook for a further 1½ hours.

Remove the paper cuff. Brush the sides with beaten egg and return to the oven for the sides to brown – about 20 minutes. When the pie is cold, fill with cooling savoury jelly.

CHOUX PASTRY

Using the basic choux pastry, you can make a
range of savoury puffs with different fillings as
well as chocolate éclairs and profiteroles.

Pâte à choux (or choux pastry as it is known here) is as French as suet crust is English. It is a decorative party pastry, light, attractive and crisp. Surprisingly it is not difficult to make.

The ingredients must be carefully measured and the flour really dry. The chief ingredient of successful choux is air, so the mixture, after the addition of each egg, must be really well beaten to introduce air as the raising agent, for choux relies on this natural lift.

Choux needs more thorough cooking than people think. If the pastry is not cooked enough, the sides will be softer than the top and the whole thing will collapse when it comes out of the oven. If the cooking is well done a natural hole will form in the centre.

Although in this country we know éclairs and cream buns best, there are all sorts of exciting things that can be done with this fascinating pastry.

What went wrong

It is important to have the right proportions in choux pastry. Measure, don't guess. If the mixture does not rise when cooking, did you think self-raising flour would be best to use? It is not – do stick to plain flour.

If it sinks when it comes out of the oven it was not cooked long enough.

A forcing bag and one or two plain pipes, 1 cm (½ inch) and 2.5 cm (1 inch) are useful items of equipment for this pastry, though not essential.

CHOUX PASTRY

150 ml (¼ pint) water
50 g (2 oz) butter
pinch of salt
65 g (2½ oz) plain flour
2 eggs

Heat the oven to 220°C (425°F) mark 7. Put the water, butter and salt into a saucepan. Bring to the boil. Continue boiling until all the butter has melted. Sieve the flour on to a piece of paper. Remove the pan from the heat and tip the flour in all at once. Mix well and beat thoroughly with a wooden spoon. Return to very low heat, beating well until the mixture forms a ball and leaves the side of the pan. Remove from the heat at once.

Cool a little and add by degrees the beaten eggs, beating all the time. A hand-held electric mixer is good to use. You may not need all the second egg. The mixture should look satiny and drop heavily from the spoon.

Cook for 10 minutes then reduce the temperature to 190°C (375°F) mark 5 and continue for a further 30 minutes, or according to the recipe.

Éclairs, profiteroles and so on should be put straight on a wire rack to cool, out of the draught. A slit should be made in the side of each, with a sharp pointed knife, to let out the steam so that the inside will dry.

Sweet choux can have a little caster sugar put into the original recipe with the water. Savoury choux should be well seasoned with salt and pepper at the beating stage.

SAVOURY PROFITEROLES

Makes 18

65 g (2½ oz) choux pastry (see
  page 86) with salt and pepper
  added
25 g (1 oz) butter
25 g (1 oz) plain flour
275 ml (½ pint) milk
pinch of nutmeg
salt and pepper
1 tsp chopped parsley
200-g (7-oz) can salmon

Heat the oven to 220°C (425°F) mark 7.
Prepare the shelves and baking sheets and
cook the profiteroles exactly as for Curry
Puffs (see page 89). When they are cooked
and cool, fill with the following mixture.

Melt the butter in a pan. Stir in the flour
and cook over a low heat for 1 minute.
Remove from the heat and add the milk by
degrees, beating continuously. Return to
the heat, bring to the boil, and simmer for
2–3 minutes stirring all the time. Add a
pinch of nutmeg and seasoning to taste. Put
into a bowl and stir in the chopped parsley.

Remove all bones and skin from the
salmon, flake it, and fold into the parsley
sauce. Enlarge the slit in the sides of the
profiteroles and fill with mixture, using a
teaspoon, very carefully and neatly.

For alternative fillings see below.

HAM FILLING

100 g (4 oz) cooked ham
50 g (2 oz) apricot chutney
50 g (2 oz) butter
pepper

Mince the ham. Stir in the chutney and
butter and season to taste with black
pepper.

CHICKEN FILLING

100 g (4 oz) cooked chicken
50 g (2 oz) butter
salt and pepper
½ tsp Worcestershire sauce

Put the chicken through the fine blade of
the mincer. Beat in the butter, season well
and stir in the Worcestershire sauce until all
is well blended.

POMMES DE TERRE DAUPHINE

Makes 10–12

450 g (1 lb) potatoes, boiled
salt and pepper
25 g (1 oz) butter
1 egg
deep fat for frying
65 g (2½ oz) choux pastry (see
    page 86)

Sieve the boiled potatoes, season, and beat in the butter and egg. Heat the fat. Mix the choux pastry and potato mixture together. Beat with a wooden spoon and season well. Put as much as you can handle comfortably into a forcing bag fitted with a 1-cm (½-inch) plain pipe.

Pipe 2.5-cm (1-inch) lengths one by one on to a damp tablespoon. Slip gently into hot fat. Fry until the potato is honey coloured. Remove with a slotted spoon on to absorbent kitchen paper. Keep hot whilst frying the remainder and serve at once.

This is a culinary conjuring trick. The choux comes to the outside, leaving a soft centre of rich potato.

SAVOURY ÉCLAIRS

Makes 18

65 g (2½ oz) choux pastry (see
    page 86) with salt and pepper
    added
100 g (4 oz) smoked salmon
3 tbsp béchamel sauce (see page 11)
lemon juice
black pepper

Heat the oven to 220°C (425°F) mark 7. Grease and flour two baking sheets. Fill a forcing bag fitted with a 1-cm (½-inch) plain pipe. Pipe 6-cm (2½-inch) lengths on to the baking sheets, keeping well apart.

Cook for 10 minutes then reduce the temperature to 160°C (325°F) mark 3 and continue for a further 20–30 minutes until a warm honey brown and well risen. Slit the sides and cool on a wire rack out of the draught.

Mash the salmon with a fork. Stir in the béchamel sauce and season well with lemon juice and black pepper. Split the éclairs in half. Fill the bottom halves with the mixture and replace the tops.

CREAM CHEESE ÉCLAIRS

Makes 18

65 g (2½ oz) choux pastry (see
    page 86) with salt and pepper
    added
60 g (2 oz) shelled walnuts
100 g (4 oz) cream cheese
½ tsp homemade mustard (see
    page 74)

Heat the oven to 220°C (425°F) mark 7.
Prepare the shelves and baking sheets and
cook the éclairs exactly as for Savoury
Éclairs (see previous page).

Chop the walnuts finely. Stir into the
cream cheese with the mustard. Split the
éclairs in half. Fill the bottom halves with
the mixture and replace the tops.

Savoury éclairs, after being filled, are
sometimes finished with a brushing of aspic
jelly sprinkled with finely chopped salted
almonds.

CURRY PUFFS

Makes 16

65 g (2½ oz) choux pastry (see
    page 86) with 1 rounded tsp curry
    powder added with the flour
100 g (4 oz) cream cheese
1 rounded tsp finely chopped
    gherkins
paprika

Heat the oven to 220°C (425°F) mark 7.
Arrange two shelves in the top half of the
oven. Grease and flour two baking sheets.
Drop or pipe the pastry on to the baking
sheet, either with a teaspoon or in a forcing
bag with a 1-cm (½-inch) plain pipe. Keep
the pieces of dough well apart.

Cook for 10 minutes then reduce the
temperature to 160°C (325°F) mark 3 and
continue for a further 20–30 minutes until a
warm honey brown and well risen. Cool at
once on a wire rack out of the draught.
Make a little slit in the sides of each to let
out the steam. Mix the cream cheese and
gherkins together. Cut each choux bun in
half and fill with the mixture. Replace the
top half and dust with paprika.

If a teaspoon is used to drop the pastry on to
the baking tray, dip it in water after each
bun is formed. The pastry will then slip off
easily.

POLKAS

Makes 16

65 g (2½ oz) choux pastry (see page 86)
75 g (3 oz) apricot jam
1 small lemon
275 ml (½ pint) crème pâtissière (see page 32)
icing sugar

Heat the oven to 200°C (400°F) mark 6. Grease two trays of deep tartlet tins with butter. Line the tins with choux pastry. A wet teaspoon does the trick. Bake in the top half of the oven for 5 minutes, reduce the temperature to 160°C (325°F) mark 3 and continue for a further 10 minutes or until the little cases are a warm honey brown.

Remove gently from the tins on to a wire rack. Sieve the jam with the zest and juice of the lemon. Put a teaspoon of the jam into each polka, fill with crème pâtissière and dust with icing sugar.

In days gone by the icing sugar was thickly powdered and was then 'touched by a red hot flat iron'.

CHOCOLATE ÉCLAIRS

Makes 12

65 g (2½ oz) choux pastry (see page 86)
275 ml (½ pint) whipping cream
25 g (1 oz) caster sugar
75 g (3 oz) plain chocolate
225 g (8 oz) icing sugar
2 tbsp hot water

Heat the oven to 200°C (400°F) mark 6. Arrange two shelves in the top half of the oven. Grease and flour two baking trays. Pipe 9-cm (3½-inch) lengths of choux diagonally on to the baking sheets, leaving plenty of room between them. Use a forcing bag fitted with a plain 1-cm (½-inch) pipe.

Cook for 20 minutes then reduce the temperature to 160°C (325°F) mark 3. Reverse the position of the trays in the oven and cook for a further 20 minutes. Make a small slit in the side of each éclair and cool on a wire rack.

Extend the slit and fill with whipped cream sweetened with caster sugar.

For the chocolate icing: break up the chocolate and put in a basin. Stand the basin in a pan of hot (not boiling) water.

Sieve the icing sugar into a bowl, add the 2 tablespoons of hot water and stir until well mixed. Add the softened chocolate and beat until glossy. Cover the top of each éclair with chocolate icing from the tip of a spoon and leave to set.

Coffee icing can be used as an alternative to chocolate. Dissolve 4 tablespoons instant coffee in 1 tablespoon hot water and gradually beat into 225 g (8 oz) icing sugar until smooth.

CHOCOLATE PROFITEROLES

Serves 6

65 g (2½ oz) choux pastry (see
    page 86)
275 ml (½ pint) whipping cream
1 tsp caster sugar

Chocolate Sauce
175 g (6 oz) good dark chocolate
1 tsp cornflour
salt
25 g (1 oz) butter
25 g (1 oz) caster sugar

Heat the oven to 220°C (425°F) mark 7. Arrange two oven shelves in the top half of the oven. Grease and flour two baking sheets. Make as for Savoury Profiteroles (see page 87). Cool on a wire rack. Make small slits in the sides to let out the steam.

Whip the cream stiffly with the caster sugar. Using a forcing bag with a 1-cm (½-inch) plain pipe, fill the choux buns with the cream. Pile up into a dish.

For the chocolate sauce: melt the chocolate in a bowl over hot water then stir 75 ml (3 fl oz) water into it. Mix the cornflour and salt with a little water in another bowl. Bring 50 ml (2 fl oz) water to the boil. Pour on to the blended cornflour, stirring all the time. Return to the pan, cook for a minute or two, then add the chocolate mixture to the cornflour sauce. Beat in the butter and sugar. It is important to keep stirring until the sauce is made. Just before serving, pour the warm chocolate sauce over the profiteroles.

PARIS-BREST

Makes about 10

65 g (2½ oz) choux pastry (see
  page 86)
2 tbsp flaked almonds
275 ml (½ pint) crème pâtissière (see
  page 32)
2 tbsp praline (see below)
icing sugar

Heat the oven to 200°C (400°F) mark 6.
Arrange two shelves in the top half of the
oven. Line two baking sheets with baking
paper. Put the choux pastry into a forcing
bag with a 2.5-cm (1-inch) plain pipe. Pipe
out circles about 7.5 cm (3 inches) across.
Sprinkle with flaked almonds and dust
lightly with icing sugar.

Cook for 15 minutes, reduce the
temperature to 190°C (375°F) mark 5 and
continue for a further 20 minutes.

Put on to a wire rack and make a little slit
in each to let out the steam. Cool. Split in
half carefully and mix the crème pâtissière
with the praline and use to fill each little
circle. Replace the tops and dust a little
icing sugar over the almonds on the tops.

This can be made in the form of one single
larger ring, about 18 cm (7 inches) in
diameter. Use 65 g (2½ oz) choux pastry
and a 4-cm (1½-inch) plain pipe. 275 ml
(½ pint) crème pâtissière will be sufficient
to fill it.

PRALINE

75 g (3 oz) unblanced almonds
75 g (3 oz) caster sugar

Put the nuts and sugar in a heavy saucepan.
Melt over a low heat. When turning pale
brown stir with a metal spoon until nut
brown. Pour on to an oiled slab or baking
sheet. When cold, pound or crush with a
rolling pin. Store in an airtight jar.

PARTY RING

Serves 6

65 g (2½ oz) choux pastry (see
   page 86)
275 ml (½ pint) whipping or double
   cream
4 ripe peaches
100 g (4 oz) icing sugar
peach food colouring
angelica

Heat the oven to 200°C (400°F) mark 6. Put
the oven shelf in the top half of the oven.
Grease an 18-cm (7-inch) sandwich tin with
butter. Put the pastry into a forcing bag
fitted with a 2.5-cm (1-inch) pipe. Pipe a
ring of pastry around the edges of the tin.
(This is an easy way of making a choux
ring.)

Cook for 20 minutes. Reduce the
temperature to 160°C (325°F) mark 3 and
continue for 20–25 minutes until the ring is
a warm honey brown. Cool on a wire rack.
Make a small slit in the side to let out the
steam.

Whip the cream stiffly. Take care if using
double cream not to end up with butter.
Dip the peaches in boiling water. Skin them
and cut into small pieces. Fold into the
cream. Split the ring in half. Fill the bottom
half with the peach mixture and replace the
lid. Make the glacé icing with the icing
sugar and approximately 2 tablespoons
water faintly tinged with peach liquid food
colouring. Pour the icing over the ring and
decorate sparingly with angelica diamonds.

The pastry ring can be made in the morning
or the day before. Put it into an absolutely
airtight tin when cold. It can then be filled
just before the party.

WHAT IS THE WI?

If you have enjoyed this book, the chances are that you would enjoy belonging to the largest women's organisation in the country — the Women's Institutes.

We are friendly, go-ahead, like-minded women, who derive enormous satisfaction from all the movement has to offer. This list is long — you can make new friends, have fun and companionship, visit new places, develop new skills, take part in community services, fight local campaigns, become a WI market producer, and play an active role in an organisation which has a national voice.

The WI is the only women's organisation in the country which owns an adult education establishment. At Denman College, you can take a course in anything from car maintenance to paper sculpture, from book binding to yoga, or cordon bleu cookery to fly-fishing.

All you need to do to join is write to us here at the **National Federation of Women's Institutes, 39 Eccleston Street, London SW1W 9NT**, or telephone 01-730 7212, and we will put you in touch with WIs in your immediate locality. We hope to hear from you.

ABOUT THE AUTHOR

Janet Wier is a City and Guilds trained cookery teacher and taught the cake icing and sweet-making courses at the WI's Denman College for several years. She is a WI National Cookery Judge, Demonstrator and Assessor. She belongs to Bramshaw WI, is a past County Chairman and Voluntary County Market Organiser of Hampshire. Other books by the author include *Can She Cook?*, *Cook – Yes She Can* and *Cooking for the Family*.

INDEX